SEMINOLE PATCHWORK

Margaret Brandebourg

SEMINOLE PATCHWORK

Sterling Publishing Co., Inc.   New York

Published in 1987 by
Sterling Publishing Co., Inc.
Two Park Avenue
New York, N.Y. 10016

ISBN 0-8069-6610-6 hardcover
            6616-5 paper

First published in Great Britain in 1987.
Published in the United States by arrangement with
B.T. Batsford Limited, London.
This edition available in the United States,
Canada and the Philippine Islands only

Printed in Great Britain

Contents

Acknowledgements

I would like to thank Dr Jonathan King of the British Museum, Museum of Mankind, for his initial help, and for allowing me to photograph the collection of garments at the museum (Figure 11 and colour plates 1, 3, 4, 9a, 9b, 9c and 9d). Also Mrs Barbara Stuckenrath and Dr W.C. Sturtevant of the Smithsonian Institution, Washington D.C. (Figures 1, 2, 16 and colour plates 2 and 7) and Daniel O. Markus of the Metro-Dade Cultural Centre, Florida for making available their collections of photographs. Special thanks are due to Alec and Fiona Peever for their help with all the other photography, and to Imogen Winter for her general assistance in the production of this book. The two photographs reproduced in the introduction are supplied courtesy of the Historical Association of Southern Florida.

Chapter One

A brief history of the Seminole Indians

The story of the Seminole Indians of Florida is one of adaptation after years of persecution by the colonists. Their original home was Georgia and Alabama — they were known as the Creek Nation — but when the Europeans started to settle along the Atlantic coast during the early 1700s the Indians were driven farther south ahead of them. Always willing to trade with the French, English and Spanish settlers they resisted all attempts to enslave them. The colonists had to rely on slaves from Africa to do the hard manual labour in the forests and on the farms. Although the Indians shared the same culture, rituals and ceremonies, there were two distinct language groups, neither of whom could understand the other. Moving south into the Spanish territory of Florida they tended to settle alongside those groups who spoke the same language. About 1750 some of the Creek Indians settled near the present city of Gainesville where they were joined by other tribal groups. It was at about this time that the white men began to call the Indians 'Seminole', regardless of language, location or tribal group. This word, of uncertain origin, is thought to mean 'wild' or 'undomesticated'. The present day Seminole is a heterogeneous blending of Indian tribal groups

In 1763 Spain ceded Florida to England. It remained English for twenty years; this was a time of peace and prosperity for the Seminole. They owned large herds of cattle and horses and farmed the land with great skill. During this time runaway black slaves from the plantations across the border were allowed to live with the Indians in freedom. In 1783 Florida was returned to Spain. The Seminole continued to flourish until the white settlers became incensed at the sanctuary offered by the Indians to their slaves. Attempts by the slave owners to re-possess their slaves resulted in their being regarded as foreign invaders by both the Spaniards and the Seminole; this attitude angered

the American Government and resulted in a full scale retaliation in 1812, when the government sent an army into Seminole territory. The Indians resisted this attempt and the army was forced to retreat, but worse was to follow. A reprisal organised in 1813 used mounted cavalry and other army units to invade the territory with specific orders to 'chastise the Indians, plunder and burn their homes, destroy their crops and confiscate their cattle'. This foray proved more successful and the Seminole fighting spirit was temporarily crushed, their homes in ruins and their cattle and horses scattered. From 1816 onwards many incidences of bloodshed between the federal forces and the Indians is recorded, triggered off by the persistent demands from the Southerners for the return of the slaves being harboured by the Seminole. After much fighting and pillaging of Indian towns and villages the Seminoles and Creeks were forced to move further south in Florida in 1818.

The American Government bought the entire Florida territory from Spain in 1819. General Andrew Jackson was appointed military governor of Florida in 1821, in spite of, or because of his well-known prejudices against the Seminole. But because his harsh policies did not get enough support he soon resigned.

The Seminole, who had been dispersed further south in 1818, now began to recover their strength and re-organize themselves into permanent villages located on rich lands suitable for the pursuance of their expertise in farming and husbandry. One must assume that the success with which their efforts were rewarded once again led the white man to covet this rich and fertile land for development. A council was held at Moultrie Creek in 1823 to negotiate with the Indians for their land. Seventy Indian chiefs were told that they would have to move yet again from their villages to the interior of the country below Tampa Bay. Not all the Indian chiefs would agree to sign this treaty, so the long standing conflict over land and slaves continued.

In 1832 the same Andrew Jackson, but now President Andrew Jackson, ordered all the Indians to leave Florida altogether and re-settle in the Indian territory known as Oklahoma. Attempts were made to resolve matters but to no avail. The Indians were unwilling to leave their homes and villages again, so the American government entered into the most protracted and expensive Indian war, lasting seven years. The superior numbers and organization of the armed forces led the Seminoles to fight an evasive war which was finally concluded in 1842 by agreement. A small number of the Seminoles refused to sign any agreement, and these survivors, perhaps as few as three hundred out of five thousand, took refuge in the sub-tropical regions of the Everglades. Except for these few fugitives the rest of the Florida Indians had left Florida by 1860. It is only to those few that remained living in isolation in the Everglades that we owe our knowledge of the technique of patchwork now known by their name.

The struggle over slavery between North and South America, resulting in the Civil War, accounts for the isolation of those Indians that remained and their largely unknown history from that time to the beginning of this century – a period of fifty or sixty years.

So many men had been killed during the years of fighting that the family structure was dominated by women to a greater extent than before, and it fell mainly to them to build a new life in the swamp land of the Everglades. Even today the Seminole are a matriarchal society. The woman is the head of the family, owning all the property and cattle and equipment. Inheritance rights come from her side of the family. The men, however, are the decision makers in tribal affairs and she has little say in these areas. But her importance in the internal and domestic affairs of her family is supreme.

After the initial move to Florida (mid-1700s), the traditional clothing of buckskin and leather had given way to more porous fabrics acquired from traders, and made into loose-fitting garments more suitable for the hot and humid climate in which they now lived. Since the south had become the greatest cotton growing area in the world, fabrics such as calico would have been readily available, but during the Civil War cotton cloth became extremely scarce. Perhaps it was during these times that the Indians would have begun to think about the possibility of joining cloth or piecing it for reasons of economy rather than use one piece of cloth for the entire garment. This is all conjecture, however, since very little is known about their way of life and the changes that took place. It is not until the turn of the century and many major changes to the geographical location that their history becomes available again.

In 1871, on the south bank of the Miami river, the first trading post was built in the area, but the biggest change of all was the construction of the first railroad into Miami in 1896. This brought tourists and entrepreneurs to whom the Indians were pleased to sell their craft work as souvenirs, providing themselves with some cash for use in trading transactions. The introduction of the sewing machine, the old-fashioned hand-operated type, was one of the changes attributable to the railway. A couple of years later the first store was built in Miami by the son of an old Indian trader. Knowing the tastes of the Indians well, the store was stocked with bolts of bright cloth.

These two changes, the railway and a store stocked with an ample supply of bright fabric, started the women sewing in an entirely new way. Up till now they had produced appliqué and simple piecing by hand. Their ingenuity and pattern-making skills evolving at this time are responsible for the invention of Seminole patchwork, based on the use of the sewing machine and without which the whole technique becomes a nonsense. So for the first time we have patchwork designed for the use of the sewing machine.

The railway and the new roads brought tourists into the area, but it was not until the Tamiami Trail was built, in 1928, connecting Tampa on the west coast with Miami on the east coast, that the free use of the land was curtailed for the Indians. This modern highway ran directly through Indian lands, making accessible to tourists and settlers areas which had remained unknown except to the Indians. Their isolation and seclusion was now over and the freedom to use the land and waterways for fishing and hunting at an end.

The Indians are now gathered into government-owned reservations and are no longer self-sufficient. Within these reservations

Seminole Indians wearing traditional costume.

Seminole men: the man in the left foreground and the boy are wearing the traditional 'big shirt'; the others have the more modern version tucked into trousers.

Figure 1   Seminole man's 'big shirt', made in 1953;
intricate patchwork separated by bands of ric-rac braid.

they are considered a sovereign nation, exempt from some of the state laws, and subject to some of their own making. The tribal leaders have learnt to deal with the white man on his own terms. Important concessions have been granted and the Seminole tribe has now the status of a nation. The main reservations are Brighton, Big Cypress and Hollywood (formerly Dania). The Indians are mainly a tourist attraction living mostly by their crafts, since their farming skills can no longer be put to good use. In spite of this aspect of their culture they remain a rather withdrawn people within the mainly white or negro population. They guard their privacy, and still practise the festivals and ritual ceremonies of the past. The most important of these is the Green Corn Dance held annually, at which all the Seminole clans gather together to celebrate for four or five days. This marks the beginning of a new year. For these events the women still produce some of their best work, traditional costumes for their families to wear. Plates 1, 2 and 3, the photographs in this chapter and figures 1 and 2 give an idea of how their costumes would appear at these times, more or less unchanged from those worn fifty years ago.

Figure 2   Seminole woman's skirt.

Chapter Two

Basic techniques and defining terms

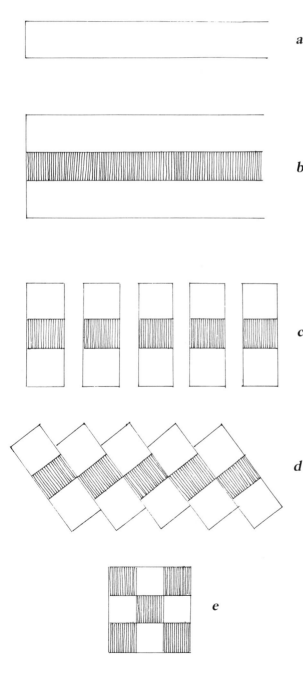

To sew long strips of fabric together, to cut them into rectangular or triangular shapes (units), and then re-assemble them into geometric patterns is the basis of the Seminole method. It will be seen from the examples of traditional dress that the strips used are extremely narrow. Such very fine work requires considerable experience and skill. For this reason I do not recommend using anything less than a 2.5 cm (1 in.) strip.

The Seminoles tore rather than cut the strips of fabric. They were assured of achieving accuracy because of the straight weave of the cloth. If a fabric has been tested for tearing straight it is worth experimenting with this method. Before starting to tear, mark the width of your strip on the selvage and clip in with scissors for about 5 cm (2 in.) then tear. Tearing fabric into strips distorts the torn edges of the fabric; the method used by the Seminoles for removing this was to hold the strip taut at either end and draw it rapidly over the edge of a table once or twice. This has the same effect as pressing but only takes a fraction of the time. Modern production of fabric is so different that one needs to cut rather than tear. The simplest way of doing this is to use card templates of varying widths. I suggest a length of 50 cm

Diagram 1
a STRIP A length of fabric which has been marked and cut to the width of the chosen template, always on the straight grain of the fabric.
b STRIP BAND Several strips of fabric which have been seamed together preparatory to cutting into units.
c UNIT A vertical or diagonal or triangular piece cut from the strip band preparatory to re-joining to form the pattern band or block.
d PATTERN BAND A repeated geometric design derived from an arrangement of units.
e BLOCK OR MOTIF A combination of two or more units to make a square or rectangular block.

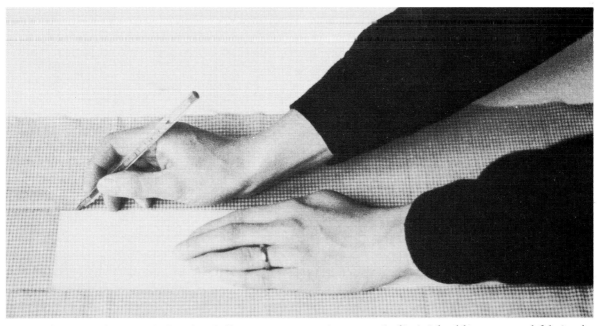

Figure 3   Fabric being marked with a ballpoint pen on either side of a template.

(20 in.) so that the template can be moved along, keeping the end within the lines already marked on the fabric. A ballpoint pen, or white pencil for dark fabrics, can be used to mark either side of the card (figure 3). A number of card templates of various widths, prepared ready to use, facilitate the initial stages of cutting (diagram 2).

All fabrics must be washed and ironed before use. In authentic Seminole patchwork plain and very bright fabrics are used. Red and yellow and bright green or blue are standard colours. Black and/or white is popular for the background. I find patterned fabrics can give a pleasing effect, and will enable variations of tone to be more readily achieved. However, a print can overwhelm or defeat the intricacy of the pattern itself; since the ingenuity of the construction is so fascinating, it is

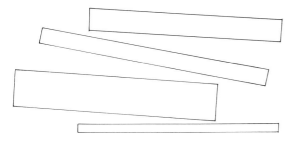

Diagram 2
A selection of card templates.

a pity to see it diminished by patterned fabric. At least to begin with your most arresting work will be achieved with plain fabrics.

Consideration of tone plays a most important part in the construction of patterns, and sometimes the alteration of the placing of tonal values can create new patterns. Three values — dark, medium and light — are usually sufficient to achieve all the effects required. The ribbon block gives an example of this (figure 4).

A good result can be marred by puckered seams. One reason for the excellence of the Seminole piecing was their use of the hand-operated sewing machine: the hole in the needle plate was small, so the fabric was not drawn down into the bobbin case to cause puckering and uneven seams. Using modern electric machines, a fine needle and fine thread are helpful, and make sure that your needle has not become blunted during use. If there is a tendency for the material to become entangled in the bobbin case, holding the fabric both in front of and behind the presser foot, keeping it quite taut as you allow it to move through, will help this particular problem.

Puckering may occur when fabrics of different weights are joined. If you are joining a lightweight and a heavier fabric, do as much sewing as possible with the lighter piece on top, where you can hold it slightly taut as you guide it through the machine.

Seam allowances should be approximately 5 mm (¼ in.). This will allow for any fraying and

15

Figure 4   Ribbon block with three tones of fabric.

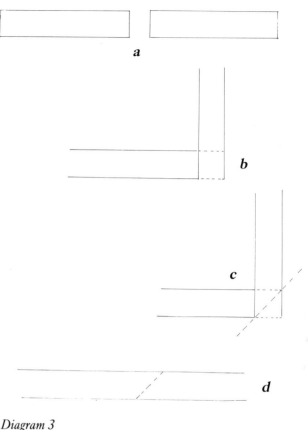

Diagram 3
a   *Two strips to be joined.*
b   *One strip placed on top of the other, at right angles, right sides together and pinned.*
c   *Marked with ballpoint pen and seamed together from upper outside edge to lower edge diagonally opposite. Outer triangle is trimmed off and pressed out flat.*
d   *Finished bias seam.*

will produce a strong result which can be washed. Even with the narrowest band recommended, the seams will only meet in the middle and not overlap. The length of strip that can be cut from any particular piece of fabric may vary a great deal, but as it is more economical to use strips of the same length it becomes necessary to join strips to equal out the length. For this purpose it is preferable to make a join on the bias. The method for doing this quickly and accurately is shown in diagram 3.

Similarly, when joining blocks to make a pattern band of diagonal squares, the method shown in diagram 4 will be both economical of fabric and satisfactory in result, because the joining triangles will be on the bias.

To cut a strip band into diagonal units can be very wasteful of fabric. Considerable saving can be effected by seaming the strips together, lining them up on the diagonal, according to the direction of the cutting line (diagram 5).

When the strips have been joined into the strip band, the result must be well pressed before cutting into units. Seams are not opened out, but pressed flat, all in one direction. When pressing the joined units it is not possible to be dogmatic about the direction of the seams, but as a general rule all seams should go in one direction, unless there is a particular reason for not doing so — such as too many seams meeting at one point resulting in bulkiness. It is interesting to note how

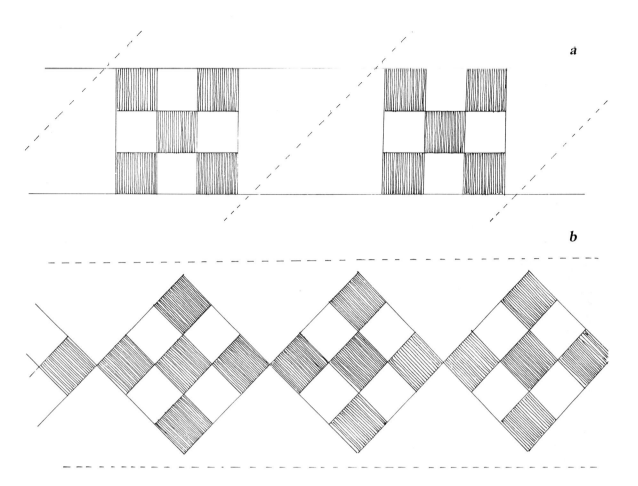

Diagram 4
a *Pieced blocks to be set on the diagonal are joined into a strip. The measurement of the section between each block is one block, plus two generous seam allowances. Cutting lines are marked from the base of one seam allowance to the top of the other. Marking and cutting continues along all sections.*
b *Join blocks. The diagonal cutting line will form the top and bottom edge of the band.*

the Seminoles turned the direction of the seam from one end of a unit to another, resulting in seams consistently twisted so that one assumes it was part of the technique. This was probably a practical method which came about because of the direction of sewing; the presser foot of the sewing machine will naturally press all seams towards the machinist. I try to avoid such twisting, so that subsequent pressing is simplified.

Before cutting strip bands into units it is important to ensure that the seams are straight. After pressing, place a ruler on the seam to straighten (see diagram 6). Using the ironing board as a table can be convenient at this stage, then the strip band can be pinned into position to prevent it curling. When a band of vertical strips is required, as in pattern band sixteen on page 43, the method shown in diagram 7 will be found useful, saving time and making for greater accuracy.

Equipment needed
The most important of the normal sewing aids that one will need is the sewing machine. The Seminole women used hand-operated models and these still have a great deal to recommend them. When the seams to be sewn are very short, in the initial stages of piecing, the greater control of the hand machine can be a help. However, longer seams are eventually required, so an electric machine makes the work less tiring.

Because different colours of fabric are used, with the seams crossing from one colour to another, it is impossible to match the thread to the fabric. I choose one that is neutral, perhaps beige or grey, instead of black or white.

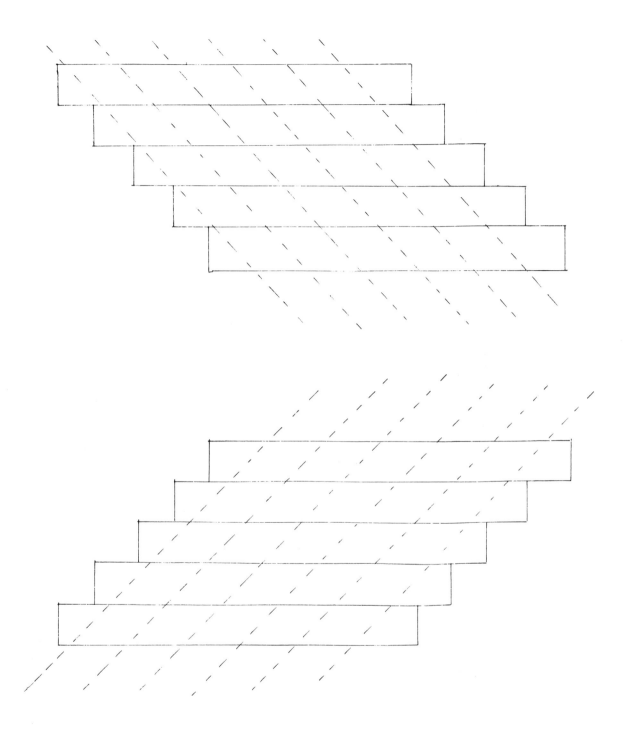

Diagram 5
Method of joining strips into a strip band to save wastage of fabric when cut into units on the diagonal.

Card templates

These have been mentioned already (diagram 2). To prepare, use a craft knife for cutting and a metal ruler to guide the knife. Lightly score with the knife along the edges of the ruler; do this several times until the card is cut through. This will minimize any accidents.

Diagram 6
a   *Template or ruler placed on seam line of strip band to straighten.*

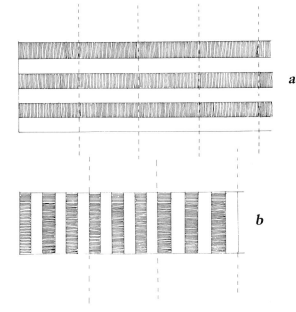

Diagram 7
a   *Strips seamed and marked into units. The units are the width of the required pattern band.*
b   *Units joined to form pattern band.*

45° Set square
Not too small; I use one with 30 cm (12 in.) sides.

Protractor
Only necessary for a few of the patterns.

Markers for fabric
An ordinary ballpoint pen is very effective. It makes a thin line without using pressure, which tends to distort the fabric. Even if the line does not wash out, it will be on the inside of the work after seaming. There are many washable fabric markers on the market but I find the line tends to be rather thick. A white pencil crayon can be used on dark fabric; this must be kept well sharpened.

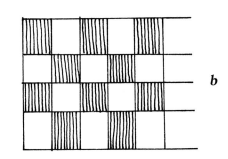

Diagram 8
a   *Template of 5 cm (2 in.) used for cutting strips and units.*
b   *Chequerboard pattern of four strips with alternate units reversed. The squares produced after seaming are 4 cm (1½ in.). The top and bottom row will become square after insertion into work.*

Having decided on a particular pattern band, it is not necessary to make allowances for seams. As long as the same amount of seaming is taken up every time, the proportions of the pattern will remain the same; but the pattern band will be a considerable reduction of the strip band, according to the number of strips and units used.

If the same template is used for cutting the strips as well as the units the resulting shapes within the pattern will be square (diagram 8). Using a 5 cm (2 in.) template throughout, the width of the finished pattern band will be approximately 15 cm (6 in.). On this four strip pattern band one has therefore 'lost' 5 cm (2 in.) in width. The amount of loss in the length will be calculated according to the number of times the unit measurement will fit in to the length of the strip band. Thus if the strip band is 25 cm (10 in.) and the width of each unit is 5 cm (2 in.), the number of units obtainable from this band will be five. After seaming, each unit will be reduced to 4 cm (1½ in.) resulting in a finished length of pattern band of 19 cm (7½ in.).

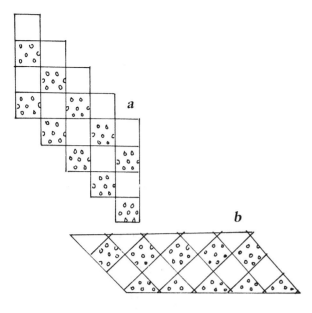

Diagram 9
a *Units seamed together before top and bottom edges are straightened.*
b *Resulting pattern band after cutting off points along both edges. The amount of loss will be equivalent to one square of the pattern.*

Diagram 10
a *Strip band with units marked using a narrower template than that used for strips.*
b *Resulting pattern band of vertical rectangles.*
c *A wider template used for unit markings.*
d *Resulting pattern band of horizontal rectangles.*

If you think that all this sounds very complicated remember that the originators of Seminole patchwork did not go in for these sort of calculations, but achieved a 'feel' for the amount of loss that would occur during seaming, simply by getting used to the method. If one wants to be less formal about measurements, an observation by one of the Seminole women — that she calculated ten yards of strip band to make up into four yards of her favourite pattern band — is quite useful. It demonstrates just how considerably the length will be reduced after seaming.

Another consideration needs to be taken into account when offsetting units. There will be a further loss of width (not length) once the triangular points at the top and bottom have been cut off straight (diagram 9). To prevent loss of pattern due to the cutting off of the top and bottom triangles, make the outside strips of the strip band slightly wider, so that when the units are assembled there is plenty of room for cutting and seaming without interfering with the pattern.

Making patterns composed of squares is the result of using the same width of template throughout. If one uses a narrower template for cutting the units than that used for the strips the resulting pattern will be composed of vertically rectangular shapes. Alternatively, a wider unit of measurement will produce horizontally rectangular shapes (diagram 10). It is from these three possibilities that all patterns are composed.

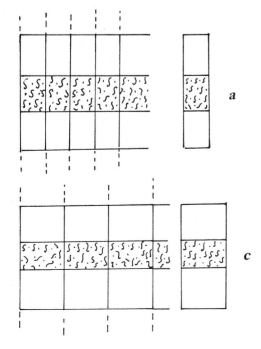

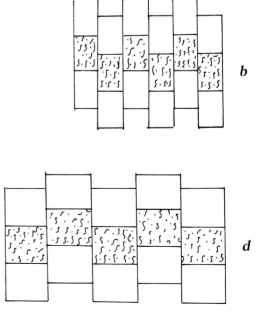

Chapter Three

Strip bands using two strips and patterns to make with them

Working with coloured paper is a good way to get the feel of Seminole patchwork. If the thought of sewing together experimental samples seems rather laborious, use firm paper to make up the strip bands and paste the units cut from them on to squared paper to make the pattern bands. Choose three papers of different tones of the same colour from which to cut the strips. For the initial patterns, strips of the same width will be required, so from each of the papers cut lengths of 4 cm (1½ in.) wide.

Make the strip bands suggested by taping the strips together horizontally and running the tape along the full length, leaving no gaps. The pieced band is now turned over and units marked out, vertically or diagonally. To make up the pattern band, paste the units on to squared paper; these can then be kept as reference samples. This is a quick method of working out new patterns for oneself. Once the first two or three pattern bands have been completed, one can then see how easy it is to manipulate cut bands into a profusion of patterns.

Indian women make pattern bands many yards long (see figure 5), perhaps 29 metres (30 yards). From this they cut off the lengths required to make up their fabrics of horizontal bands (figure 5). To make pattern bands of this length requires much joining of each strip (see diagram 3). Since fabric widths may vary, seams where the strips have been lengthened will probably not line up. This means that the seams where the cloth has been lengthened will not create too much bulk by being all in one place.

When making a long band of units it is quicker and more efficient to join them in pairs. Join two units and put aside, then another two until all the units are paired, then join the pairs to form a pattern band. Both in the pairing and joining of one pair to the next there is no need to cut the

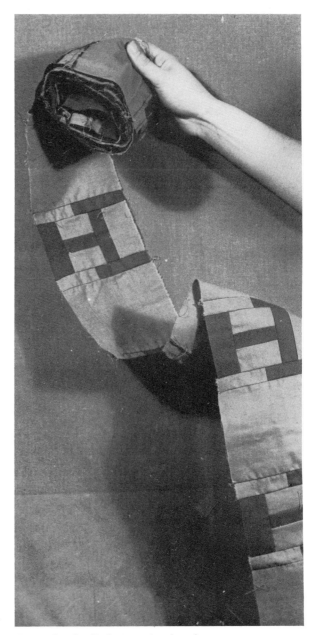

Figure 5   A roll of pattern band ready to use.

21

machine thread, each unit or pair can be fed under the presser foot consecutively and the thread between cut apart later.

Although Seminole patchwork is relatively easy in execution, it sometimes seems to be quite difficult to visualize. For this reason it is a good idea to start with a very simple pattern band.

Using a 5 cm template mark up and cut two strips from different fabrics, one light in tone and one dark. The following examples in this chapter can all be made from the same strip band, so use the full width of your fabric when cutting the strips. You will then be able to make a number of samples from this strip band to enable you to get used to this method.

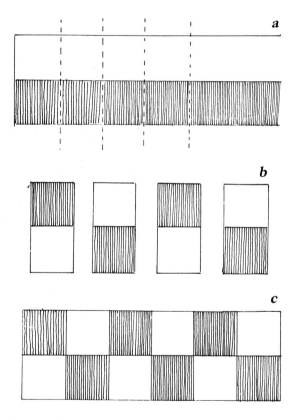

Diagram 11
a Strip band marked into units using 5 cm template.
b Alternate units reversed.
c Chequerboard-patterned strip band.

Pattern band one (*Diagram 11*)
Seam together the two strips. Using a 5 cm template, mark and cut the strip band into units.

Reverse alternate units. Seam them together to form a chequerboard-patterned strip band.

A different width of template can be used for cutting into units (see diagram 12). This will produce a band of differing proportions.

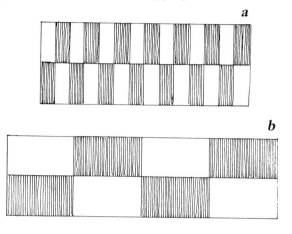

Diagram 12
a Narrower template used for cutting strip band into units.
b Wider template used for cutting strip band into units.

Pattern band two (*Diagram 13*)
A variation of the previous pattern band can be made using the same strip band cut into units as before.

Mark each unit, with right sides facing you, on the right hand edge, the first unit 1 cm below middle seam line, the second unit 1 cm above seam line.

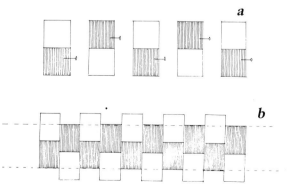

Diagram 13
a Units marked on right-hand side prior to seaming.
b Pattern band with cutting lines marked.

Continue marking alternately above and below seam line.

This pattern band has been used in the cot quilt, in figures 6 and 7, previous to the outside border.

Figure 6   Cot quilt, showing use of various pattern bands.

23

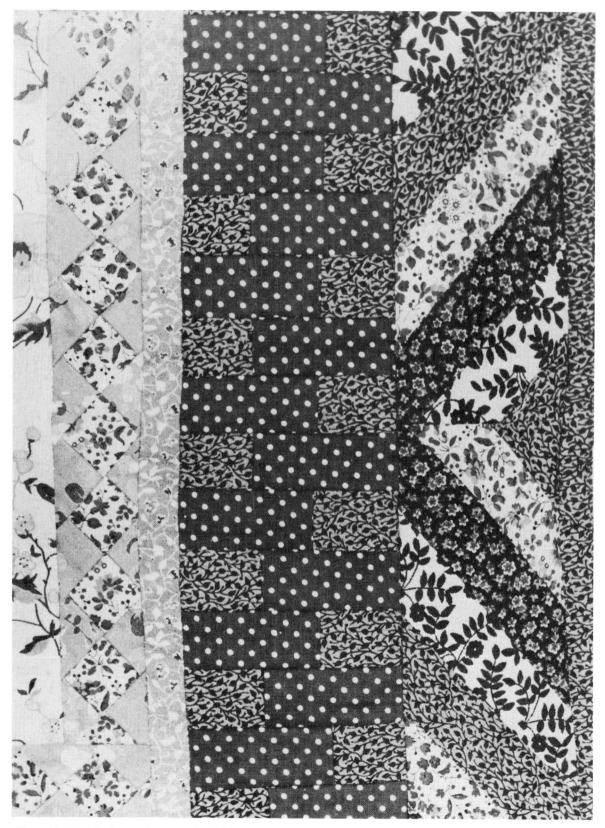

Figure 7   Detail of two strip pattern band from cot quilt.

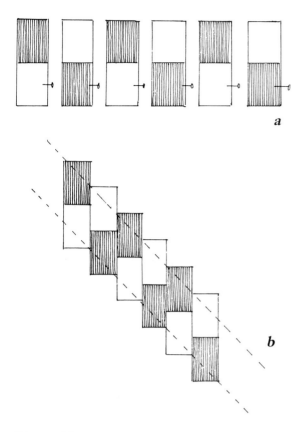

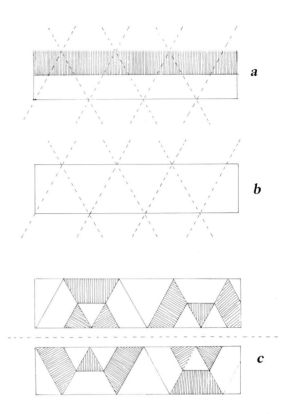

Diagram 14
a *Units marked on right-hand side prior to seaming.*
b *Seamed units with cutting line marked.*

Diagram 15
a *Two strips seamed together and marked at angles of 60°*
for cutting into triangular units.
b *One strip of background material, the same width as the*
two strip band, marked for cutting into 60° triangular units.
c *Two halves of the final pattern placed ready for seaming.*

Pattern band three (*Diagram 14*)

From the band of two strips cut units vertically.
Use a narrower template for this than the 5 cm one
used for the strips.

Re-arrange each unit to alternate in colour.

Mark the right hand side of each unit, below the
middle seam line, with the position for aligning the
units. The distance of the mark from the seam line
should be the width of the unit *after* seaming. This
will give an even line to the pattern.

Pattern band four (*Diagram 15*)

I have included the spider web strip in this
chapter, although it is possible for it to be made
with a strip band of more than two strips. The
method would be the same.

In the quilt illustrated in plate 5 you will see that
I have used the band as an all-over pattern. This is
not one of the patterns that is traditionally used by
the Seminoles but it does work out very well with
their techniques.

For the size of pattern used in the quilt you will
need two strips of differing tones, about two
inches in width. Seam these together, and
pressing the seam towards the darker of the two
colours, mark and cut the strip band at angles of
60° as shown in diagram 15a.

Six of these triangles will make one pattern.

Measure the width of the seamed strip band after seaming and cut a strip of background material the same width. Again mark into 60° angles and cut.

To assemble: take three pieced triangles, reversing the middle one, and seam together.

Now add a plain triangle on either side before continuing the strip with three more pieced triangles.

Make two strips like this and seam together to form the pattern band.

Pattern band five (*Diagram 16*)

The directions for the saw tooth pattern much favoured by the Seminoles is given in the next chapter, but a band of light and dark triangles can be made in the manner illustrated in diagram 16 if only a short band is needed. For larger projects this method would be uneconomical of material.

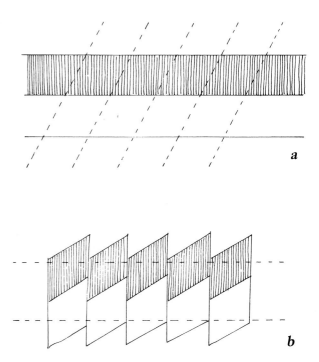

Diagram 16
a *Strip band marked at 60°, prior to cutting into units.*
b *Units seamed together. Cutting lines marked.*

Chapter Four

Three strips and more

It would be impossible to include in this book all the varieties of pattern available by using the Seminole method; there are so many, and new ones are always being invented. However, I am including many authentic Seminole patterns, as well as those that I have discovered myself.

The three-strip band can prove somewhat easier than the two-strip band, since the seam lines of the centre strip will provide points for aligning the units. Without these seam lines the alignment points must be measured and marked on each unit. Even with the three-strip band one does not always want to align the units on a seam line. The following method will save time and achieve an accurate measurement overall. When the strip band has been seamed and marked into units, cut only two of these units, to enable the exact point of alignment to be decided.

With these two units laid side by side shift them until the offset is where you want it. Where the cross seam of the right hand unit meets the edge of the left hand unit, make a mark. Using this marked unit as a guide you can now mark the rest of the strip band. This can be done with a ruler parallel to the seam line and a short pencil or pen mark on the right-hand side of each unit cutting line. The jackets in figures 17 and 19, pages 62 and 65, have been marked in this way, because the units are joined other than where two seams meet.

One of the most popular of the Seminole pattern bands is pattern band six. Different results can be attained with this method by using a number of different three-strip bands from which to cut the units, the central strip in each of the bands being a different colour. The border adjacent to the central medallion in plate 8 is an example of this, using three different colours for the central strip in each of the three bands, and using a unit from each strip band in sequence. Three is the minimum number of bands for this pattern, but any number above this can be used. One must remember that the two outer strips will be trimmed off straight after the units are joined, so that with a three-strip band only the central band will form the pattern, or with a five-strip band only the inner three, and so on. The two outer strips can merge with the other fabric to which they are joined by using similar cloth. One of the children's jackets in figure 19, page 65, uses a five-strip band with the two outer strips made from the same fabric as the rest of the jacket.

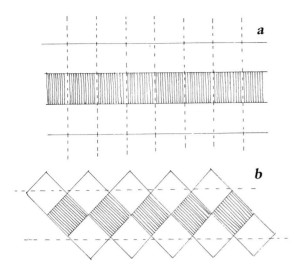

Diagram 17
a *The two outer strips are the same fabric.*
b *Units joined so that the bottom seam of one unit lines up with the top seam of the next unit. Using a straight edge as ruler, straighten both edges.*

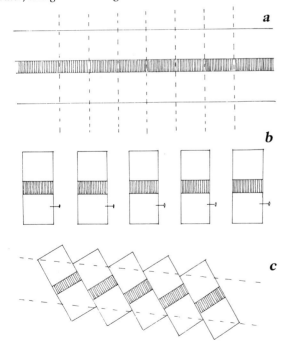

Diagram 18
a *Strips seamed together and marked vertically for cutting into units. The unit width is the same as the width of the outer strip.*
b *Units cut and marked on right-hand side for lining up with the upper seam of the middle strip.*
b *Units cut and marked on right-hand side for lining up with the upper seam of the middle strip.*
c *Units seamed together with cutting line indicated.*

Pattern band six (*Diagram 17*)
Use the same width of template to cut the strips for the strip band and the units from the strip band. Remember to keep seam lines the same, approx. 5 mm (¼ in.).

Cut three strips of equal width, two from the same fabric.

This three-strip pattern band can be varied by using a different width of template for the central strip. (See diagram 18, figure 8.) The lining up of the units into a pattern band requires some care.

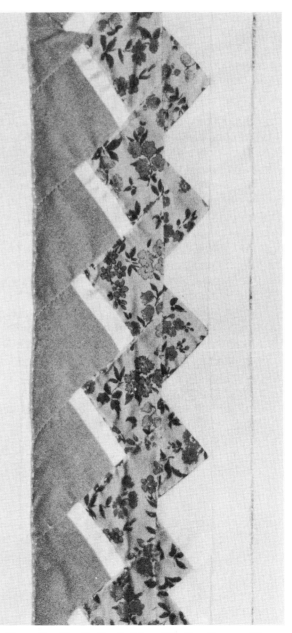

Figure 8 Detail of quilt (plate 12). See diagram 18.

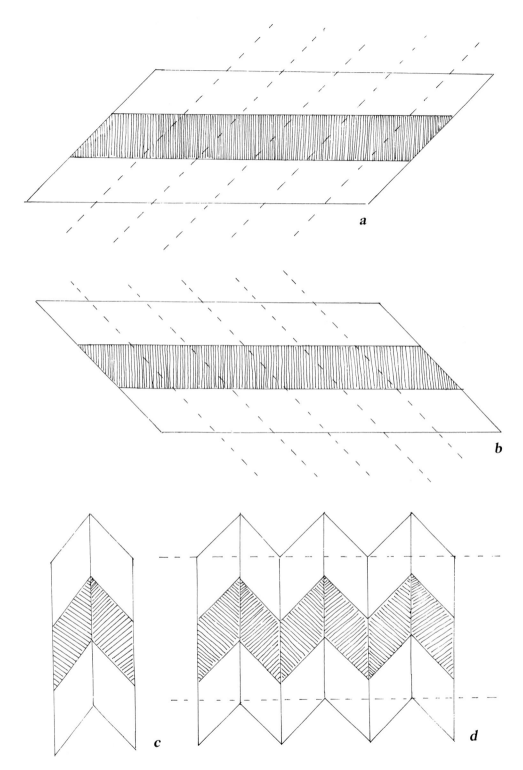

Diagram 19
a *Cutting lines at 45° for one half of chevron.*
b *Cutting lines reversed for other half of chevron.*
c *Two units seamed together to make one chevron.*
d *Pattern band of chevrons with cutting line indicated.*

Pattern band seven (*Diagram 19*)

Again, using three strips of identical width, one can experiment with chevron patterns. This pattern band requires units cut from the strip band at an angle. Units can be cut at any angle, but the most usual variation is 45° or 60/30°. In the example shown in figure 9 the angle is 45°. If a more pointed chevron is preferred the angle could be 60/30°. This pattern requires two slants of the same angle, to form each side of the chevron. To save fabric I usually make two strip bands from which to cut each angle, with the strips lined up at the angle of the cut (see diagram 5, page 18).

Slants of both directions can be cut in one operation by making one pattern band only and folding it in half. Mark only one side with the angled cutting lines, but cut through both layers, making sure that the two layers are together and

do not shift out of place as you cut. This method is very efficient, but you will be left with some triangular pieces from either end of the strip band.

Whichever cutting method you use you will need two units from the reversed angles to make one chevron (see diagram 19c).

Similar to the way in which three strip bands are the minimum for pattern band six, this is also true for pattern band seven. After this minimum number of three, the strips for the strip band can be increased to any number, bearing in mind that it becomes more difficult to be accurate with too many strips to handle.

Figures 9 and 10 show how a three-dimensional quality can be achieved using two strip bands of different tonal values. Figure 10 shows a double row of chevrons using four strips instead of three (see diagram 20). As in pattern band six (diagram 17) the two outer strips use the same fabric as that to which they are joined.

Figure 9   Detail of quilt (plate 8).

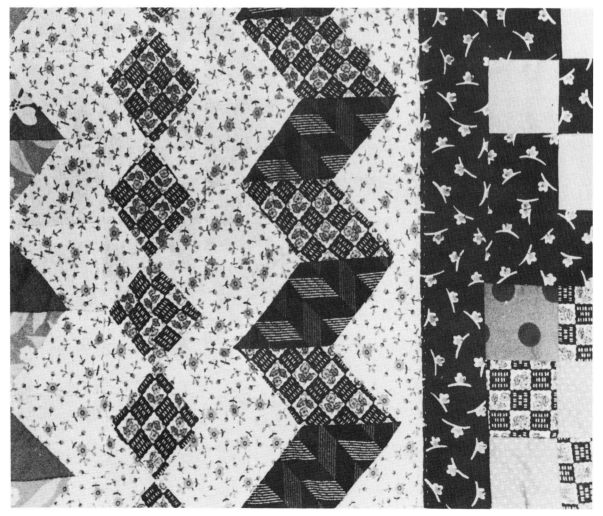

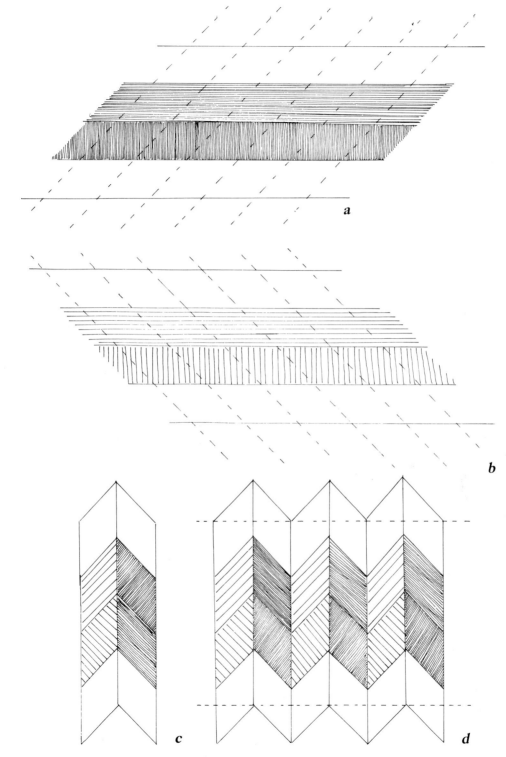

Diagram 20
a *Four strips seamed together and marked for cutting to make a double row of chevrons.*
b *The reverse angle marked on another four strips, using a lighter-toned fabric for the two central strips.*

*Figure 10   Detail of quilt (plate 8). Four strip band forms
a double row of chevrons. See diagram 20.*

1. *Seminole woman's skirt.*

2. Seminole woman's skirt.   3. Seminole man's shirt approx. 1960.

4. *Garment seams on wrong side.*

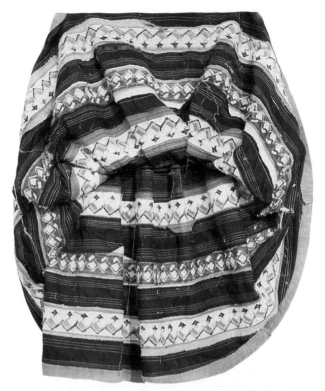

5. *'Pyjama Stripe Blues'. 250 cm × 190 cm quilt designed and made by author.*

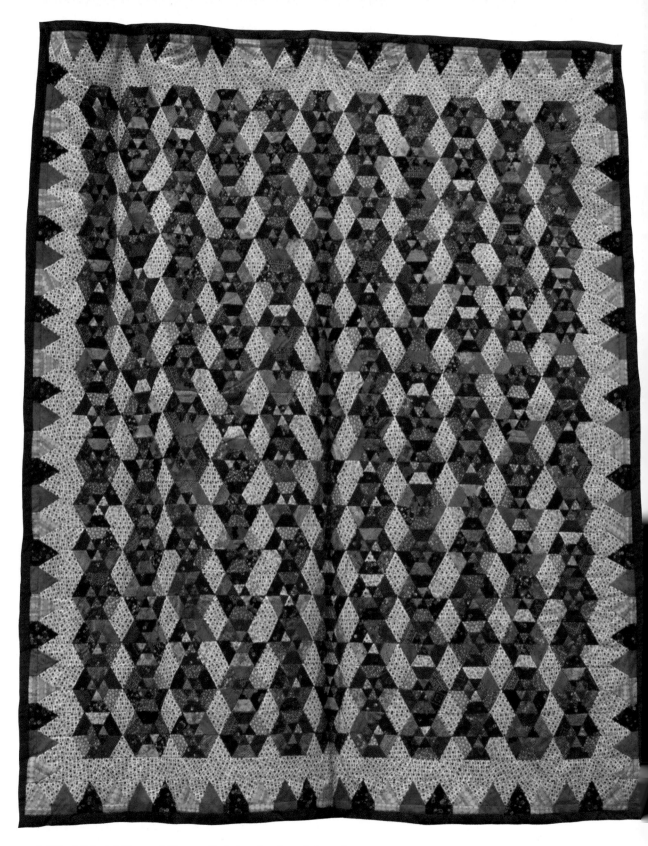

6. 'City Nights'. 251 cm × 208 cm quilt designed and made by author.

7. Detail: Seminole woman's skirt.

8. Seminole 1. 255 cm × 255 cm quilt designed and made by author.

*9a, b, c, d. Block designs exhibited at Museum of Mankind,
London, by Mary Koenes in 1985.*

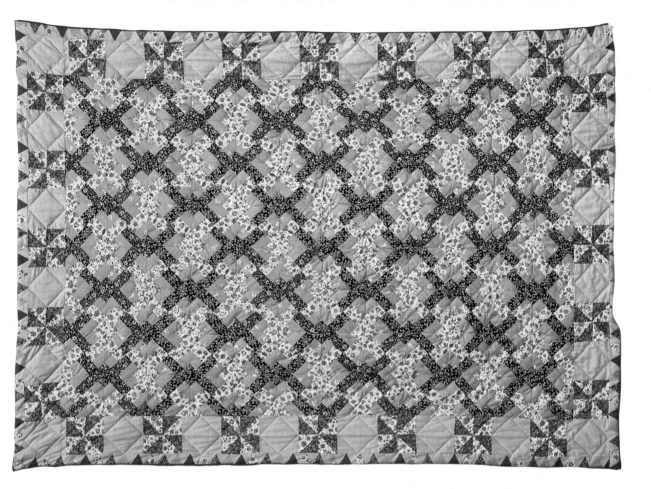

10. 'Interlacing'. 242 cm ×
169 cm quilt designed and
made by author.

11. 'Field of Gold'. 184 cm ×
170 cm quilt designed and
made by author.

12. Detail of 'Interlacing' quilt.

Pattern band eight (*Diagram 21*)

Although similar to the preceding pattern band, this particular method can be used when very long lengths are required. The units are joined lengthwise *before* the middle seam of each side of the chevrons is sewn. This makes it particularly suitable for an all-over design. As stated previously, to join too many strips together can create difficulties with accuracy. This is where the extra step (illustrated in diagram 21b and d) can be useful. I have only used six strips for the strip band. An even number of strips will prevent two of the same fabric meeting when the units are joined lengthwise.

Diagram 21

a *Six strips assembled and marked into units, preparatory to the seaming of each of the units from this section to form a long length.*
b *Two units from this section (**a**) placed ready for seaming.*
c *Reverse angle of six strips sewn and marked as before.*
d *Units from section **b** placed ready for seaming.*
e *Strips of units from **a** and **b** seamed together to form a long band of arrow-like chevrons.*

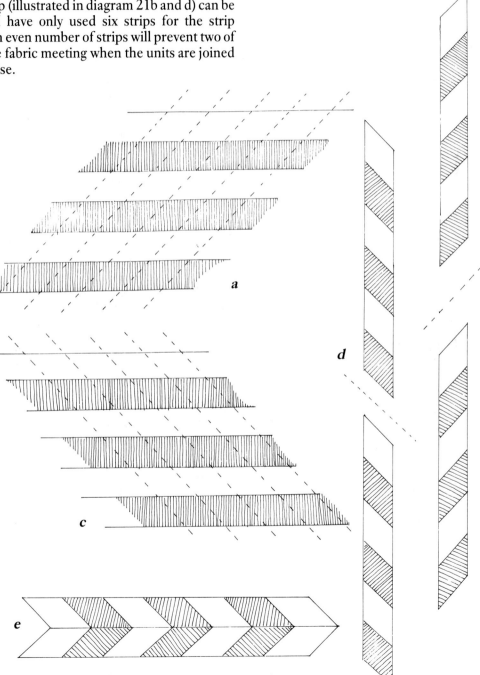

Diagram 22

a Units seamed together lengthwise, using as many units as necessary to achieve a complete length, and then seamed to its mirror image to make the first length of chevrons.
b Several lengths put together to make the required width.

The quilt illustrated in plate 6 has been made from the traditional type of men's pyjama cloth, which used to be readily available in many varieties of the familiar blue and white stripe. The fabric on either side of the chevrons is not matched up, but the stripes in the fabric help to carry the design across from side to side. (See diagram 22.) The matching up of the seams on one side of the chevron to the other can be very accurate, because the cutting angle of the units will produce fabric which is on the bias and therefore easy to manipulate.

Pattern band nine (*Diagram 23*)

As mentioned in Chapter Three, the saw tooth border is another very popular one with the Seminole; it is both dynamic and versatile. Varying the proportions will vary the pattern. When it consists of elongated triangles resembling flames, the Indians call this pattern 'fire' (see figures 11 and 12). Many variations in the size of the triangle can be made by using different angles and different widths of templates for the marking and cutting of the strip band into units.

For a short pattern band I have given instructions in pattern band five (page 26), but for larger projects the most economic use of fabric would be to use the method illustrated in diagram 23.

With practice it is possible to look at the work of the Seminole and work out for oneself the method of construction. Sometimes the design appears to be very complicated; this is quite often because more than one strip band has been used, or plain strips or bands have been mixed in with the units. Examples of this are contained in the next chapter.

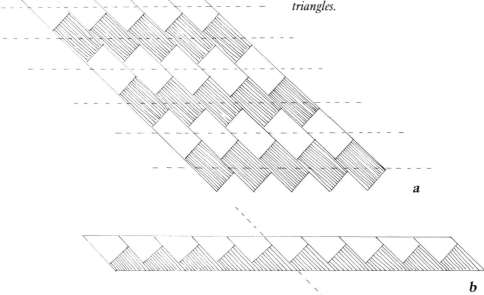

Diagram 23
a Cutting lines marked for saw tooth border on units from a strip band of six strips. Note that the cutting line has enough space on either side of it for a seam.
b Two sections of the saw tooth border seamed together. The seam allowance left on both long edges will allow the strip to be sewn without losing any of the points of the triangles.

a

b

Figure 11 Seminole child's skirt.

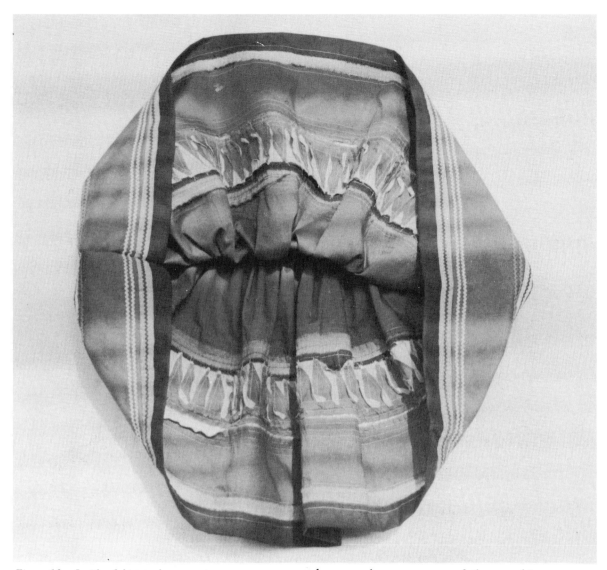

Figure 12   Inside of skirt to show seaming.

Pattern band ten (*Diagram 24*)

Only one strip band has been used for the three patterns bands in diagram 24. Each unit is cut vertically. The different results are obtained by three different arrangements of the same units. In 24b the units are offset using the middle seam line as a guide for alignment. In 24c the units are reversed before offsetting them as before. In 24d the units are reversed but not offset.

Using the same strip band as in diagram 24, diamond-shaped patterns can be made (see diagram 25). The units instead of being cut vertically will be cut at an angle. It is interesting that with the identical units from the same strip band the arrangement of the units can affect the shape and appearance of the resulting pattern band. By stepping the units upwards from left to right as in 25b the band will be shorter in length, but wider than the band produced from stepping the units downwards as in 25c.

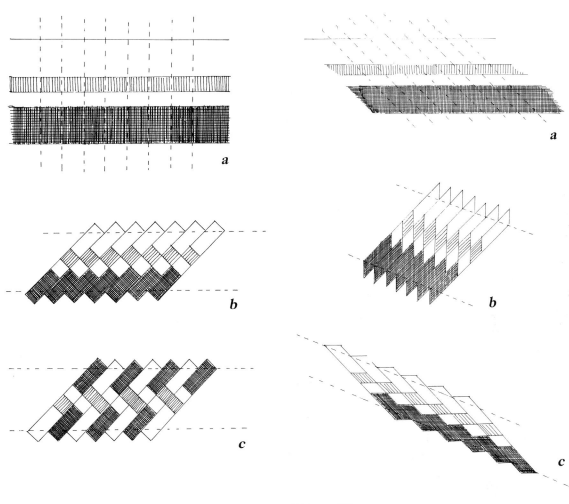

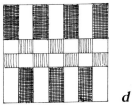

Diagram 25
a *Cutting lines for units at 45° angle, using identical strip band as that in 24.*
b *Units lined up to make band of vertical diamonds by sliding each unit upwards from left to right.*
c *Band of horizontal diamonds made by sliding each unit downwards from left to right.*

Diagram 24
a *Strip band of four strips, consisting of three different tonal values. The unit width is the same as that of the two middle bands after seaming.*
b, c, d *Three different ways of using the units from the same strip band.*

Chapter Five

Interspersing different bands

As will be seen from studying the Seminole garments illustrated, it is traditional to separate pattern bands with horizontal strips of plain fabric. These vary in width and colour so that the pattern band appears to most advantage. Black is very often used for these separating bands with white as part of the pattern band, thus providing a maximum tonal range within which the clear bright colours favoured by the Seminole do not appear discordant, and neither is the clarity of the pattern lost.

It is sometimes possible for a pattern to be constructed in more than one way, so although a particular construction is contained in the diagrams this is not necessarily the only one possible. Some constructions will be quicker to sew but perhaps take more fabric.

It has been suggested that many of the Seminole patterns have a symbolic meaning, and it is not difficult to equate some of the designs with arrows, and some with fire or lightning. These symbols are not specific to the Seminole but could be linked with the aboriginal Indians who lived in Florida before de Soto arrived with his soldiers in 1539. Symbolic patterns are found in the beadwork of these Indians and have been seen in the engravings on shells excavated in Oklahoma. By the time the present day Seminole translated such patterns into patchwork it would be reasonable to assume that most of the symbolic significance was irrelevant.

In the following pattern bands, plain unpieced units have been used in conjunction with the units from the strip band. A second strip band may also be needed to form part of the pattern of running repeats.

Pattern band eleven (*Diagram 26*)

A very simple geometric pattern. This pattern occurs in many different cultures and is sometimes known as the 'key' pattern. It requires only one strip band from which to cut one set of units, and one unpieced strip for the interspersions.

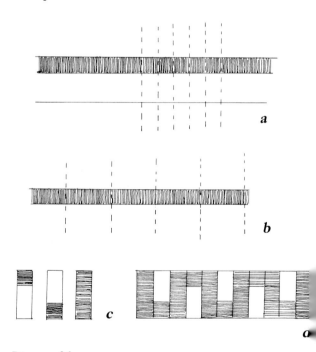

Diagram 26
a *Strip band of two strips of different tones. The darker of the two will be approximately one third of the width of the lighter one. The units are marked and cut with this narrower width of template.*
b *The same fabric as in the darker of the two strips of the strip band, and the same width after seaming. Units are cut using the same width of template as in the strip band.*
c *Two units from the strip band, with one reversed, and one from the dark strip.*
d *Reversed units arranged with a plain unit between each one as indicated.*

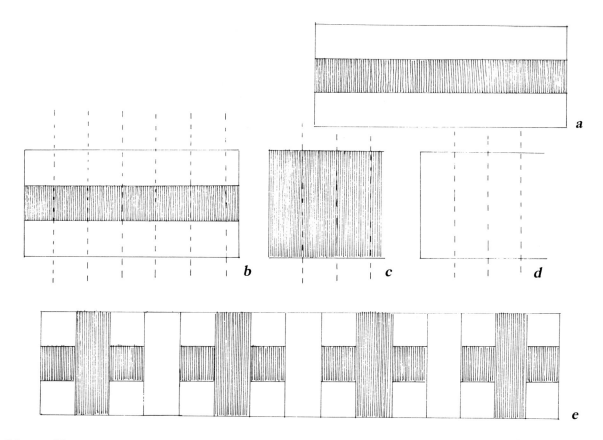

Diagram 27

a   *Strip band of three strips of equal width, the two outer strips are of the same fabric.*

b, c, d   *The strip band and two plain strips marked into units. The plain strips are the same fabric as those in the strip band. The template used for marking the unit width is the same as that used for the strips in the strip band.*

e   *Pattern band made by using one unit from the strip band interspersed alternately with one dark and one light unit.*

Pattern band twelve (*Diagram 27*)

This pattern uses two unpieced units interspersed with the units from one strip band. Sometimes cutting methods can be adapted to suit the shape and quantity of fabric at one's disposal, so although one method is indicated in diagram 27b, another method of cutting a similar unit is employed in the preceding pattern band (diagram 26c). Compare the diagrams with each other.

Pattern band thirteen (*Diagram 28*)
For this pattern two different strip bands are used with units from each one placed alternately. No plain units are added, although there is an illusory quality about the pattern which seems to suggest otherwise. Each motif on the pattern band requires three units, one from the five-strip band, and two from the three-strip band; one of the two will be reversed.

Diagram 28
a   Strip band of five strips, and one unit. The template for the unit width is the same as that used for the two middle strips. The width of the two outer strips is equal to that of the three middle strips.
b   Strip band of three strips, and two units, one of them reversed.
c   Pattern band showing three motifs.

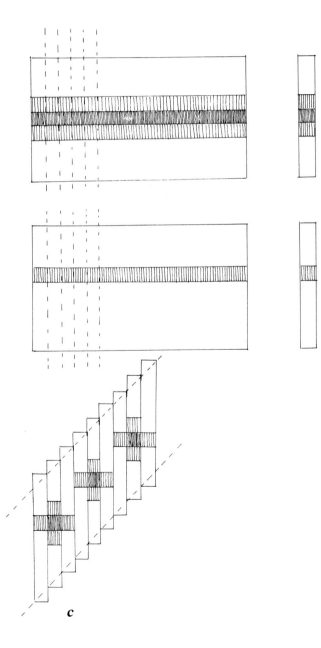

40

Pattern band fourteen (*Diagram 29*)

The pattern shown in plate 7, which is a detail from a woman's skirt, is enhanced with diamonds of ric-rac braid. The tiny crosses in the centre of each diamond are cut from one strip band with two interspersions. To achieve an even more decorative effect the maker has made a second strip band of the same proportions, but using a different colour and tone for the central strip. The units from each of these different coloured, but otherwise similar strip bands are used alternately. The pattern thus becomes more varied and interesting than it would otherwise be.

Diagram 29

a   Strip band from wide template used for the two outer light strips, and a very narrow one for the two dark strips. The middle strip is of medium width.
*b   Strip of dark fabric the same width as the strip band. Marked for cutting with the same width of template as that used for the dark strips in **a**.*
*c   Strip of light material, the same width as **b**.*
*d   Motif consisting of two units from strip band on either side of a unit from dark strip. The width of the seamed motif is measured and used to mark off units on the light strip **c**.*
e   Pattern band formed by using motifs and units from light coloured strip, with wide strips seamed to either side of this band to complete the pattern band.

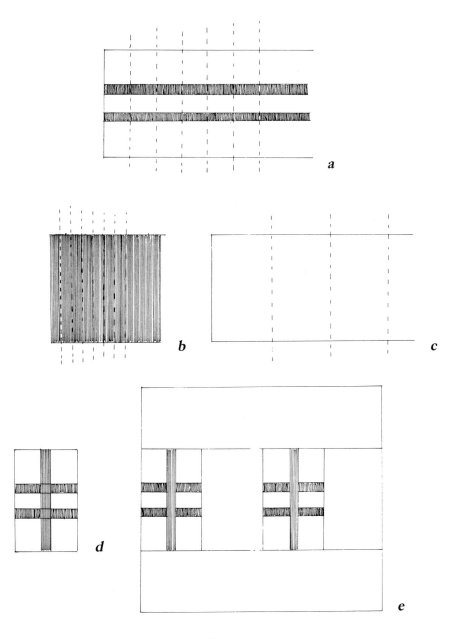

41

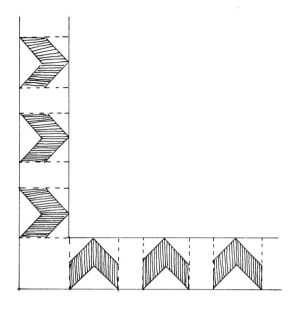

Diagram 30
a *The chevron pattern described in pattern band seven, diagram 19, interspersed with plain units.*

Pattern band fifteen (*Diagram 30*)
Using the chevron pattern explained in Chapter Four, diagram 19 (page 29), an arrow-like pattern band can be made using plain inter-spersions between each chevron. If using this band for the border of a quilt the corner can be turned with a plain square.

Pattern band sixteen (*Diagram 31*)
Another band of a composite nature, quite often found in Seminole garments. Before the addition of the interspersions further strips are added to either side of one strip band before it is cut into units. Two strip bands are needed. The width of the second strip band and the interspersions can be measured after the strips have been added to either side of the first strip band.

Traditional Seminole work is never lined or quilted, so the seam lines can be seen on the reverse side. The use of very narrow strips and units gives an impression of quilting. The extremely narrow strips seen on the surface of some Indian pattern bands are sometimes the result of a second seam being taken in after the unit has been sewn once. This results in several thicknesses of cloth overlapping at the seams. The number of seams contained in each band makes the fabric firm and thick. Sometimes the garments are sewn entirely with white thread, including the surface stitching of the appliquéd ric-rac braid. Because the number of colours used by the Seminole is so varied this does not seem to detract from the finished result.

Seminole patterns can be worked in any size. The early work of the Indian women was larger in scale than the later work which sometimes has pieces as small as 0.32 cm (⅛ in.). This gives an impression of great intricacy but also makes the pieced fabric heavy and bulky. When adapting a design to your own chosen size the main thing to remember is to keep all parts of the design in proportion to each other. Using graph paper makes this possible. Once the design has been drawn out, as in the following diagrams, assign a measurement to one square of the graph paper: this will be one module of measurement, which can then be multiplied according to the number of squares in each strip and unit. This is the most efficient way to keep the proportions correct.

In diagrams 32, 33 and 34 one can see the working out of this system. The dotted line under each pattern shows where one unit is sewn to the next. The letters between the dotted lines refer to the number of strip bands and the placing of the units. This means that all those units with the letter A will be cut from one strip band and those with B from another. P indicates a plain unit cut from an unpieced strip band.

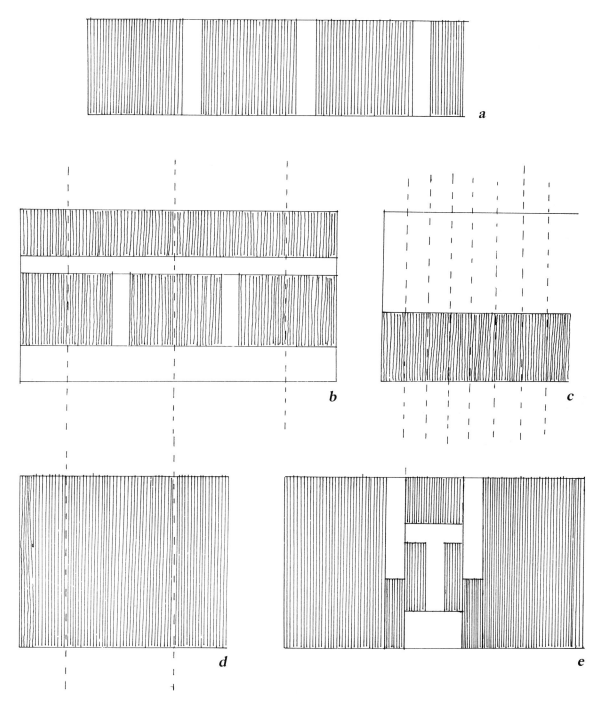

Diagram 31

a Using method described in Chapter 2, diagram 7, a band is formed of vertical strips, using two different widths of template.

b Using the proportions of the strips in the diagram, a dark and a light strip are seamed to top of band **a**, and a light one to the base. Units are cut midway between each dark section as indicated by the dotted lines.

c After measuring the width of band **b**, two strips are seamed together to make this width after seaming (note proportions used in diagram). Units are cut using narrower template from strip band **a**. These units are seamed on either side of each unit from **b** to form motif.

d A plain band of the same width as **b** and **c** cut into units of the same width as **b**.

e Plain units from **d** placed either side of motif to form pattern band.

43

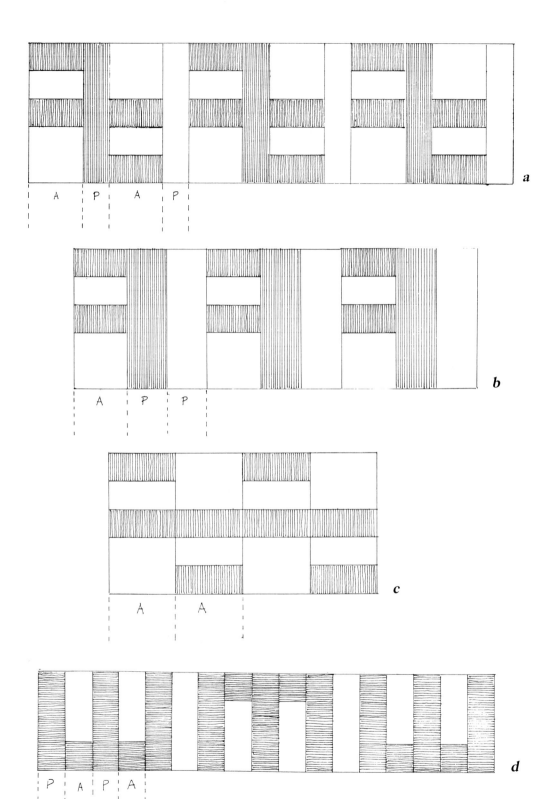

Diagram 32
These four diagrams make use of only one strip band (referred to as A) from which to cut the units. These units are all cut vertically and used alternately reversed, or in conjunction with plain unpieced interspersions, referred to as P.

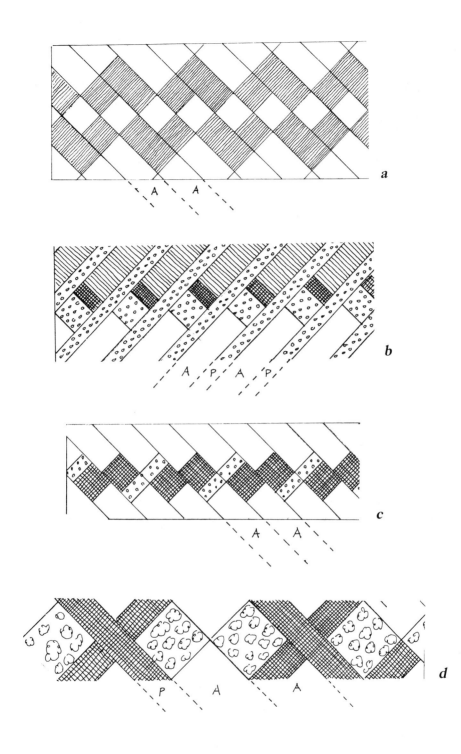

Diagram 33
These four pattern bands again use only one strip band (A),
but the units are cut at an angle, and once again used either
reversed or with plain unpieced interspersions (P).

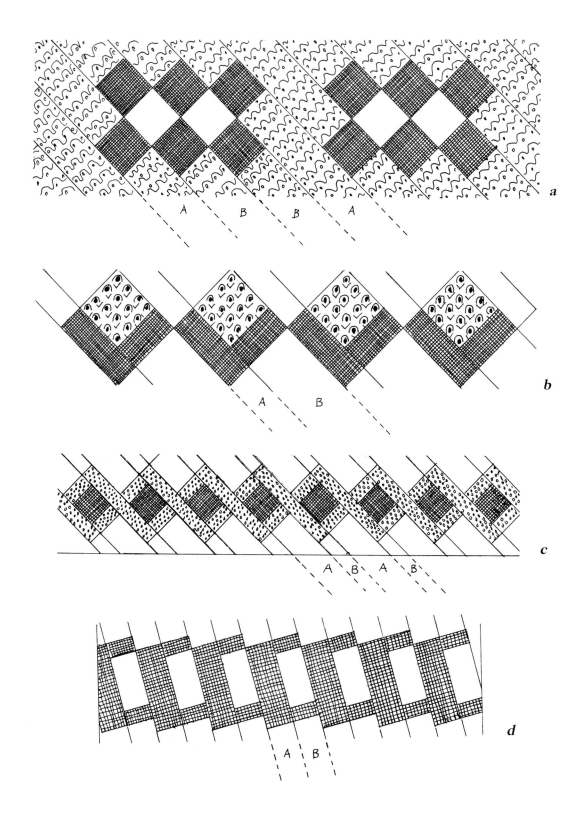

Diagram 34
All these pattern bands require two strip bands, referred to as
A and B. All the units are cut at an angle.

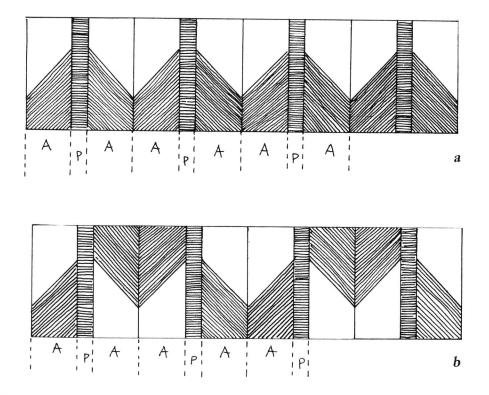

Diagram 35
Only one strip band for this pattern band with the cutting
angle reversed as in diagram 5.

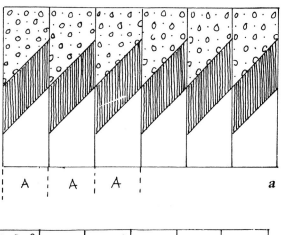

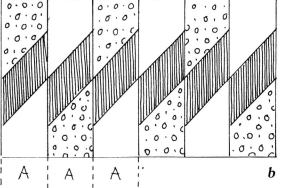

Diagram 36
A straightforward three strip band. The offsetting of each
unit makes the pattern.

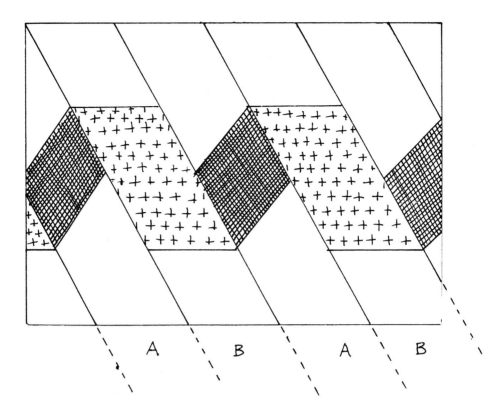

Diagram 37
Two strip bands give this folded ribbon effect; very useful for quilt borders.

In the first example, 32a, only one strip band A is needed. Each unit from this strip band is placed alternately with a plain unit P. The alternate reversal of each unit and the use of one dark and one light plain unit forms the pattern.

In diagram 32b, two plain units are used to every one from strip band A. The two plain units are of different tones to correspond with the fabric used in the strip band.

When working out measurements for 33a it will be found necessary to subtract a seam allowance for the largest of the two dark strips, since this strip is required to line up with the smaller dark and light squares. I find it easier to seam the two smaller strips together and use this as the measurement for the larger one. The occasions when one has to take into account allowances for seams occur when a larger strip has to be the same width as several smaller ones. I find it always makes for greater efficiency if the seaming of the smaller strips is done first, and then used as a measurement for the larger one. Note the examples in Diagram 34b, c and d.

In diagram 35a and b one strip band is used cut on the diagonal. Two directions of the diagonal are needed (see diagram 5).

Chapter Six

Block patterns

Many traditional block patterns can be made as well as other newer ones, by using the Seminole method.

A very simple block, resulting in a mitred square, can be cut from one strip band of three strips. This block cannot really be included as

Diagram 38
a *Three strips of equal width joined and marked into triangles at angles of 45° ready for cutting.*
b *Four triangular units seamed together to form one block.*
c *When four blocks are sewn together, a secondary pattern is created.*

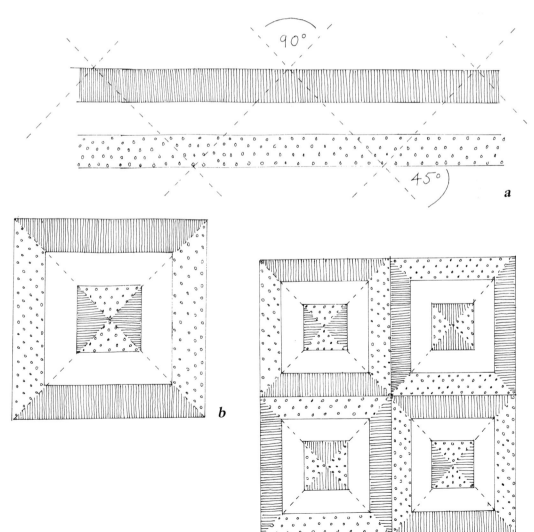

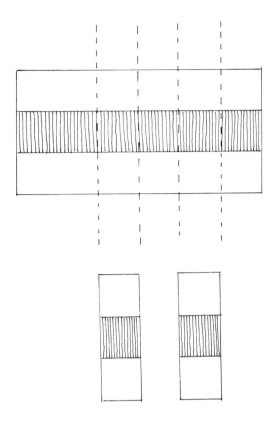

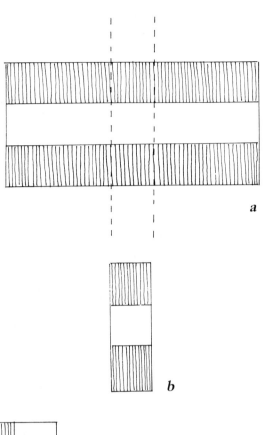

a

b

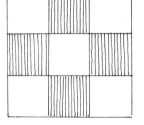

c

Diagram 39
a *Two strip band of three identical width strips. One strip band will be the opposite in tonal values to the other. Units are marked with same template as used for strips.*
b *Two units from one strip band, and one from the other will make one block.*
c *Three units make one nine patch block.*

specifically Seminole but falls within the category of strip piecing. The strip method was used by the colonists for making quilts and it may be that the Indians learnt this method via the negro slaves who came to them for refuge. In that way it is not difficult to see the origins of the work of the Seminoles. Although there is an overlap of techniques the strip method as such does not reach such dizzy heights of complex geometric pattern making until the Seminole garments of the twentieth century. With such differences in mind I have included the two examples of such strip methods in this chapter. The mitred square, diagram 38, shows four blocks set together thus making a secondary pattern on the diagonal. This simple block is worth experimenting with, either singly or on an all-over design. Used singly it could be made with different coloured strip bands, enabling one to use a more varied colour range. One way of setting it would be on the diagonal (see diagram 4, page 17) with plain blocks.

During the last ten years the block has been a developing feature amongst the Seminole. A central square, made from one or more strip

Figure 13 Nine patch block. Part of the block has become absorbed into the background by the use of the same material. See diagram 39.

Figure 14 Nine patch block with wider central strip to give a more open effect. See diagram 40.

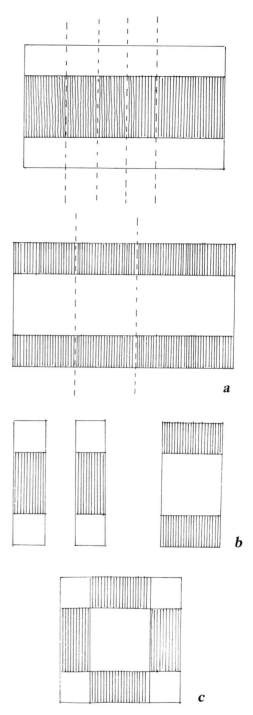

a

b

c

Diagram 40
a Two templates are needed for these strip bands, the wider one is used for the centre strip in both strip bands.
b Two units cut from one of the strip bands using the narrower template, and one from the other strip band using the wider one.
c The wider unit is placed in the centre of the block with the narrower one on each side.

bands, is surrounded by additional strips to build up a complex pattern structure. Perhaps the most useful block is the nine patch, both as a central square to be incorporated with further extensions, and on its own, either set diagonally or at right angles to the main design (see diagram 39). Tonal values, always of great importance when planning a pattern, can be used quite simply to make part of the block disappear into the background, or stand out from it. See figures 13, 14 and 31. It is also possible to vary the proportions of the block by using two templates of different widths (diagram 40). This gives a more open look. A comparison of figures 13 and 14 illustrates the difference of emphasis due to the tonal values, as well as the change in proportion of the block when using one template which is wider than the other.

Using one or other of the nine patch blocks described in diagrams 39 and 40, very intricate blocks can be planned using the 'Log Cabin' or 'Courthouse Steps' method of construction. These methods have gained popularity since the 1960s and recent work by the Seminole can be seen in plate 9. It is typical of the Indian women that every strip added is seen as a further possibility to add pattern to match and extend the pieced centre, resulting in blocks of dazzling complexity. Diagram 41 gives an example of the Courthouse Steps method of construction around a nine patch block. The variations of this method are endless, enabling much ingenuity to be used in dealing with tone and proportion. Using the same Courthouse Steps method of construction and a central nine patch block, diagram 42 gives two variations.

We return to the strip method of piecing in the quilt illustrated in plates 10 and 11. As with the other strip technique shown in the mitred square, the block which I have called interlacing needs only one strip band of identical width strips (see

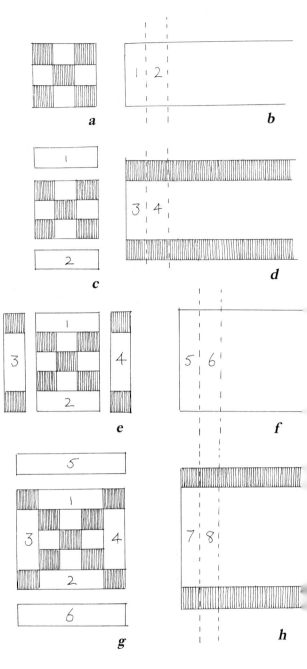

Diagram 41
a *Nine patch block to use as centre.*
b *The width of the nine patch block is used to make a template for strip **b**. Two units are cut from this strip using same template as that used for nine patch block.*
c *The two units from strip **b** are placed in position before seaming.*
d *Another strip the same width as **b** with two strips seamed to either side which are the same width as the strips used for the nine patch. Two units marked off using the latter width.*
e *Two units from strip band **d** placed in position before seaming.*
f *Use the measurement of the block for width of this strip. Two units are cut, the same width as **b** and **d**.*
g *Two units from **f** placed in position.*
h *Identical strip as in **f**. A strip is seamed either side, the same width as in **d**.*
i *Completed block with last two units added.*

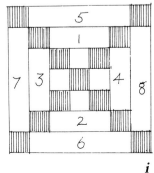

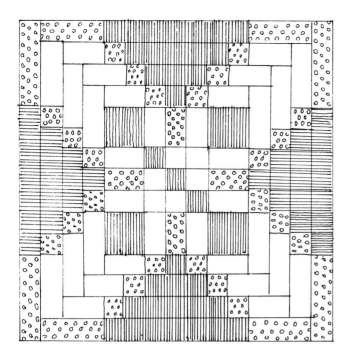

Diagram 42
*Some blocks that can be made, using a nine patch block for
the centre, and the Courthouse Steps method of construction.*

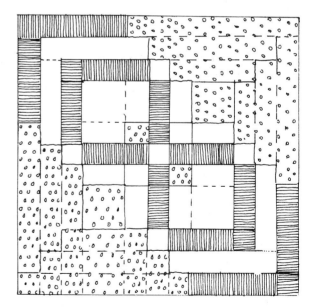

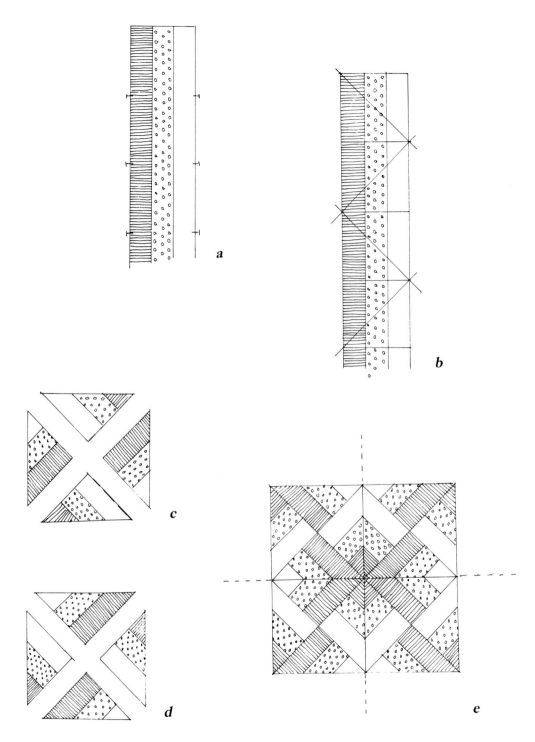

Diagram 43

a Choose fabrics of dark, medium and light tone. Keeping the width the same, strips are cut from each, seamed together and pressed. The top edge is straightened and width of band measured. This measurement is marked off on each side of the band as indicated.

b Diagonals are drawn in, the direction alternating from side to side as in the diagram.

c, d The two different blocks that can be made. Block **c** is made from four triangles with diagonals from left to right; block **d** from four triangles with the diagonals from right to left.

e Four of these blocks will make one pattern unit, two of **c** and two of **d** placed as indicated.

diagram 43). The pattern produced reminds one of a woven structure. The actual width of the strips used in the quilt before seaming was 5 cm (2 in.)

The ribbon block, shown in figures 4 and 15, is a variation of the chevron border, directions for which are given in diagram 19 (page 29). The three-dimensional quality of the blocks results from the use of two different tonal values in each of the central strips of the strip bands needed. Four chevron units (two from each strip band) will form one block.

Figure 15   The ribbon block used as the centre of a quilt (plate 8). Three different tones of fabric give a three-dimensional effect. See diagram 19.

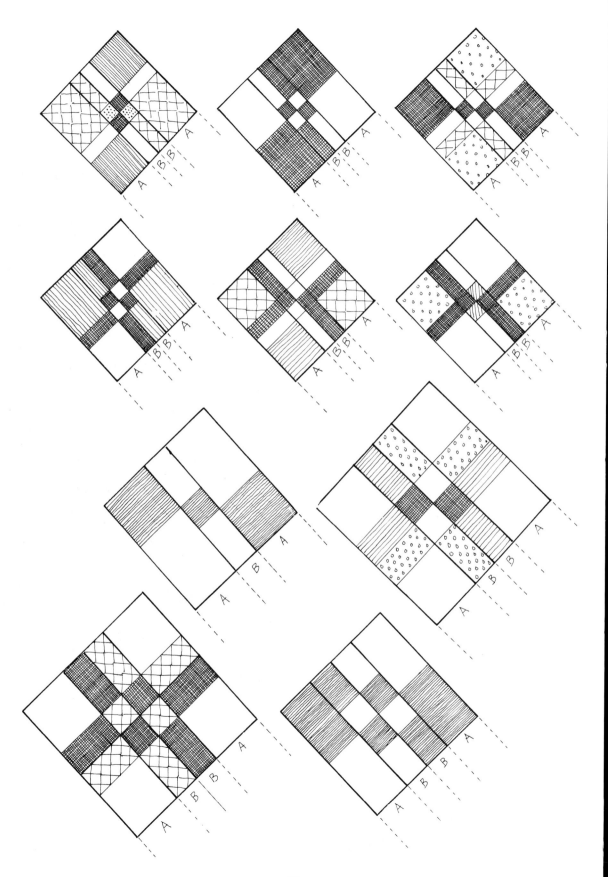

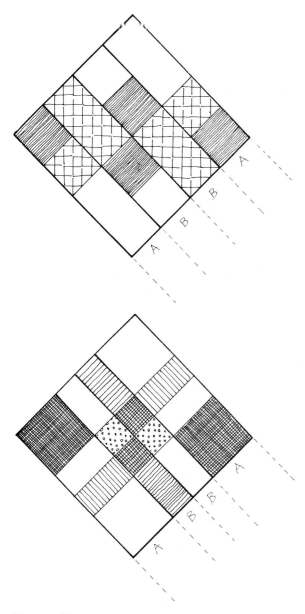

Diagram 44
For these twelve patterns two strip bands only are required,
referred to as A and B. The dotted lines show the sewing lines
of one unit to another. The letters between the dotted lines
indicate from which strip band each unit was cut.

As already stated, the development of the block
has become more complex in recent years, and the
block itself larger, using strip bands surrounding a
central square. Previous to the use of this method
the technique for making block patterns was
equivalent to that used for a pattern band. Units
from several strip bands are arranged side by side
to form a symmetrical block. Many different
variations can be achieved in each block by
different juxtapositions of the fabric. In some
cases part of the block can be assimilated into the
background by the use of the same fabric, and
other parts emphasised with fabric of different
tonal value. Examples can be seen in the woman's
skirt in plate 2, and the man's shirt in figure 1
(page 12), as well as in the central square of the
quilt in plate 12. It is customary for the Seminole
to set the blocks on the diagonal (diagram 4, page
17). The following patterns are all based on those
found in Seminole garments.

In diagram 44 only two strip bands are needed,
A and B. The number of times a unit from each of
these two strip bands is used for each block can be
understood from the letters within the dotted
lines. The dotted line indicates where each unit is
joined to the next.

Diagram 45 shows blocks made from three strip
bands, A, B and C. Two or three strip bands are
the most usual number from which to construct
this type of block; only very occasionally will four
be used.

To adapt these patterns to any chosen size
involves keeping all the parts in proportion to each
other. To do this one needs to work from the
smallest shape (usually a middle square).
Counting this as one module of measurement all
the other shapes will be either the same, or
doubled or trebled etc. The use of graph paper
will be found very helpful to work out the relative
sizes of strips and width of unit from each strip
band. Keeping all parts of the pattern in
proportion to each other, it is then possible to
make the blocks any size. Once the right
proportions have been worked out, the actual
sewing itself is formed by the reversal of units
from the strip bands.

Unlike some of the pattern bands the units are
always cut at right angles and do not involve any
re-aligning. What appear to be complex patterns
only require care in the placing of the fabrics, so
that some parts of a unit will merge with its
neighbouring unit.

Diagram 45
For the next twelve patterns, three strip bands are necessary:
A, B and C. The units required from each strip band are
indicated by the letter between the dotted line.

58

Chapter Seven

Clothes

By 1900, hand-operated sewing machines were available to the Seminole women. They had long been making clothes of colourful cotton cloth, both print and plain. Geometric appliqué and simple piecing all by hand had been used for decoration, but with the introduction of the sewing machine they began to experiment with new ways of making patterns. The transformation took place entirely in the decorative aspects of the patchwork: the cut of the pattern for the garments did not change. The distinctiveness of Seminole clothing developed during their early period of isolation; throughout this time cloth was obtained from traders. Although the first store in Miami was built in 1898 it was not until the road through the Everglades from Miami to Tampa was opened in 1928, known as the Tamiami Trail, that the Indians had access to big stores for their cloth. Then their love of bright colours became unrestrained by availability. The strips from which the patterns are made became smaller, and the patterns themselves very intricate over the years. Figure 1 (page 12) shows a shirt known as a big shirt because of the skirt-like portion. These big shirts were the traditional dress of the Seminole men, worn without trousers. The completed Tamiami Trail (1928) brought the Indians into more contact with whites, and it may have been their example which led most of the Indian men to begin wearing trousers. The skirt of the big shirt was often tucked into trousers. This practice resulted in the development of the 'transitional shirt' which had a patchwork top and sleeves, but a skirt of plain fabric. An example is shown in figure 16. It took less time to make, and there was less bulk to tuck in, but it could still be worn with trousers. By the 1940s the shirt had lost its skirt altogether and become the modern shirt, still with full blouse and sleeves but short and with a waistband. The type of pattern pieces used for this shirt are set out in diagram 46.

For the Seminole women, the period 1935 to 1940 was the highest point of fashion. Their hair was combed over enormous frames, quite easily mistaken for hats since the shape resembled a large hat brim. Many strands of beads were worn high and close around the neck. This period also became a high point for the invention of new patterns for patchwork; patterns became smaller and more complex. The tourist boom of the 1940s changed the attitude of the women to their work: more and more of them sewed for the tourist centres, leaving less time for making garments for their families. In the early 1950s collars were added to men's shirts and they were used more as jackets than shirts. (See plate 3.) The shape of men's clothing changed more than women's through the years. It has been thought that one important influence on the type of 'big shirt' worn by men can be traced back to 1736 when a group of Scottish Highlanders settled near the Indians and both lived harmoniously with each other. Of all the colonists, only the Highlanders wore skirt-like garments rather than trousers. The bright colours of the squares and rectangles of the Scottish tartans must have been observed and liked by the Indians. The impression made by seeing the Seminole in their traditional dress is one of dazzling vibrancy of colour, such as is not found elsewhere in ethnic clothes. The idea that browns, rusts and ochres are Indian colours is a mistaken one. The bright clear colours are such as would be found full strength in a paintbox. The use of black as a background to set off these colours enhances their brilliance. When designing patterns the background colour can be carried through as one of the colours in the pattern. This can create the impression that parts of the pattern

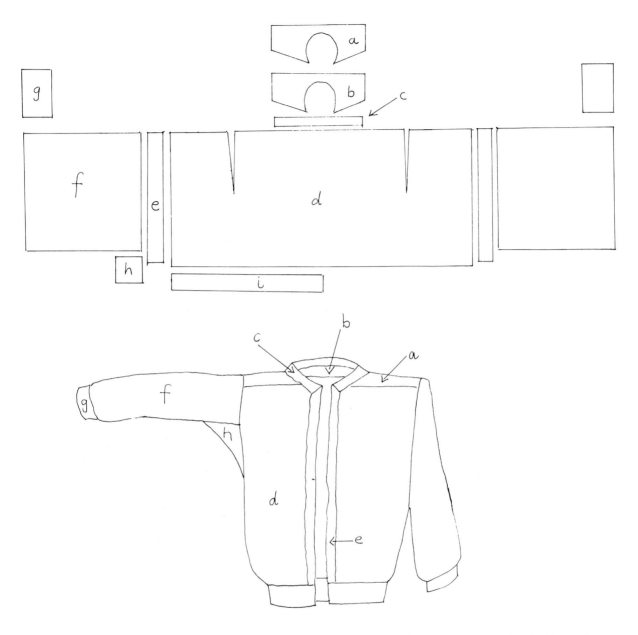

Diagram 46
Traditional pattern pieces similar to those used for man's shirt, plate 3. The shirt is assembled according to placement of pieces indicated.

are floating in space. Study the lower pattern band in the woman's skirt in plate 1 for an example of this, also the big shirt in figure 1.

No written record of the Seminole range of patterns has ever been made; the women exchange ideas in the same way as we might exchange recipes, so no design is exclusive to any one person. Sometimes an individual's work can be recognised simply by the frequency with which a favourite pattern occurs in her work. It has been suggested that years ago the lower band on a woman's skirt indicated her clan, but it is not difficult to see how this association of a pattern with a particular person might have come about. The women who sewed for their families would have made up pattern bands of great length which would have been used several times for a new garment until the length was finished. This probably gave the impression that a particular pattern was exclusive to one family. In all

*Figure 16   Seminole man's transitional shirt, with plain
lower section to tuck into trousers.*

Seminole garments there are no darts or tucks, only gathers. This is perhaps the most important point to remember when using Seminole methods to produce clothing: any darts or tucks would disturb the pattern sequence and be too bulky.

In the sleeveless jacket in figure 17 all the shaping is contained in the side panels. The method I have used to produce the patterned fabric is described in pattern band 6, diagram 17

Figure 17 Sleeveless jacket, shaping contained in side panels to avoid darts or tucks. See diagram 47.

(page 28). Instead of three strips, the fabric contains thirteen. This number can be adjusted to the length required. When all the strips have been joined together, cut into units, and rejoined, the resulting shape will not at this stage be a convenient one for use with a paper pattern. This can easily be rectified by cutting the pieced fabric through at right angles to the top and bottom edges, and re-joining to form a rectangle (see diagram 47).

Again, using a paper pattern with no darts or

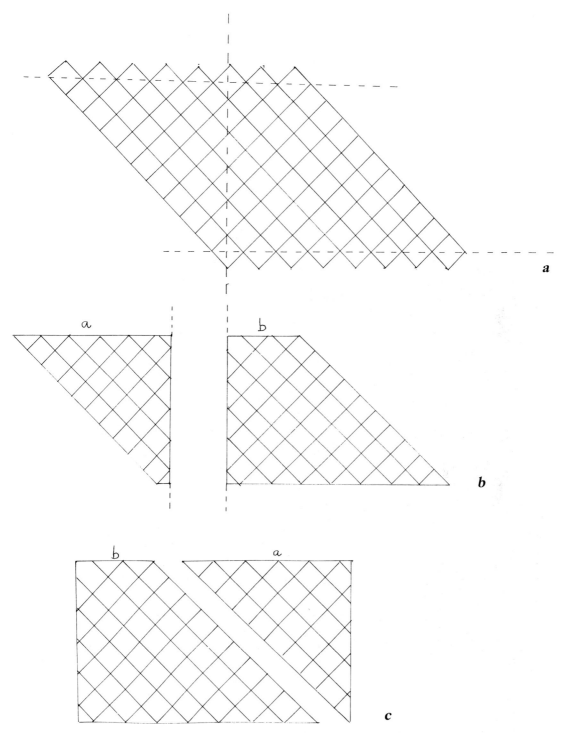

Diagram 47

a   *Top and bottom edges straightened by cutting across the triangles along the dotted line. At right angles to these lines mark and cut straight through the fabric.*

b   **a** *and* **b** *are the two pieces after cutting. These two pieces are switched so that the diagonals are adjacent.*

c   *The two pieces* **a** *and* **b** *placed ready for seaming.*

Figure 18   Sleeveless jacket, made entirely of pieces of silk scarves. See diagram 12.

tucks, the fabric for the jacket in figure 18 makes use of the method described in pattern band 1, diagram 12 (page 22). Made entirely of strips cut from old silk scarves the pattern is a simple one, but a richness of effect is achieved because of the diversity of colour and pattern contained in the scarves.

The two children's jackets in figure 19 contain no side seams and there is therefore no interruption of the pattern from the back round to the two fronts. See diagrams 17 (page 28), and 47.

After using Seminole techniques to make garments or quilts it is inevitable that one will have some scraps left over of strip bands or units or blocks etc. I keep all these pieces to use in a form of crazy patchwork, assembling them with a plain fabric. The bag illustrated in figure 20 shows one result of this method; freehand patterns of machine quilting give additional textural interest. The two small pincushions in figure 21 utilize a single block to make a decorative item.

Figure 20   Crazy patchwork bag made from pieces of strip bands and patterns left over from other work.

Figure 21   Two pincushions, each made from one block. See diagram 44.

Figure 19   Two children's jackets with no side seams. See diagrams 17 and 47.

*Figure 22   Seminole doll, made from tree bark, wearing
traditional clothes. Height 28 cm (11 in.).*

Now that the Seminole live in reservations in Florida, the once self-sufficient Indians are obliged to seek other sources of income than that afforded by farming. Tourist centres equipped with tribal stores sell patchwork and other crafts to bring in much needed money. There is an American Indian gift shop at Miami International Airport, as well as a Seminole Indian village with an arts and crafts centre a few miles north of Miami at a place called Hollywood (formerly Dania). Many other Indian villages along the Tamiami Trail, west of Miami, can be found with shops selling craft work. One of the most popular of the items is a range of dolls dressed in traditional clothes. These dolls, like the one in figure 22, are made from tree bark collected locally, and in themselves are of very simple construction, being just a column without arms or legs, but providing a shape to display the colourful clothes. Even the ways the women used to dress their hair over large frames is indicated. Smaller items for sale tend to be more popular than the traditional skirts and jackets, although these are available. The same scope for displaying the many pattern bands can be found in the aprons for sale. Diagrams 48-50 are sketches of examples of these

48

Diagrams 48, 49, 50
Examples of the aprons containing different pattern bands
now being made and sold by the Seminoles.

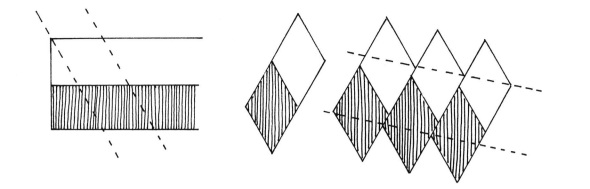

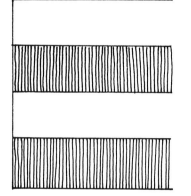

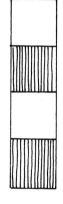

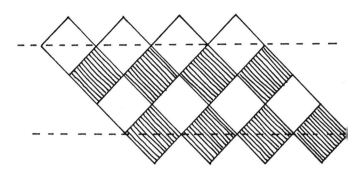

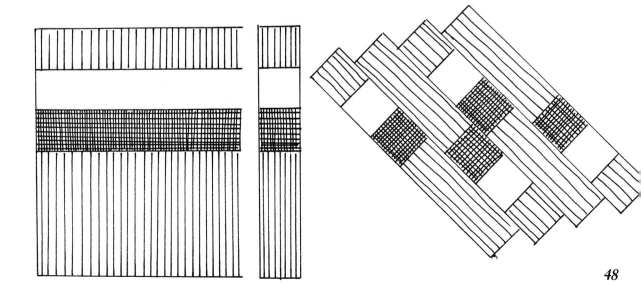

48

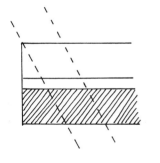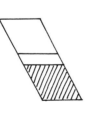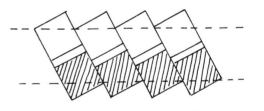

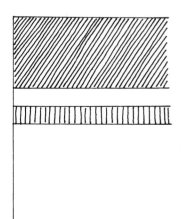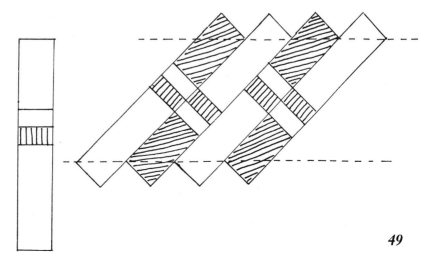

49

69

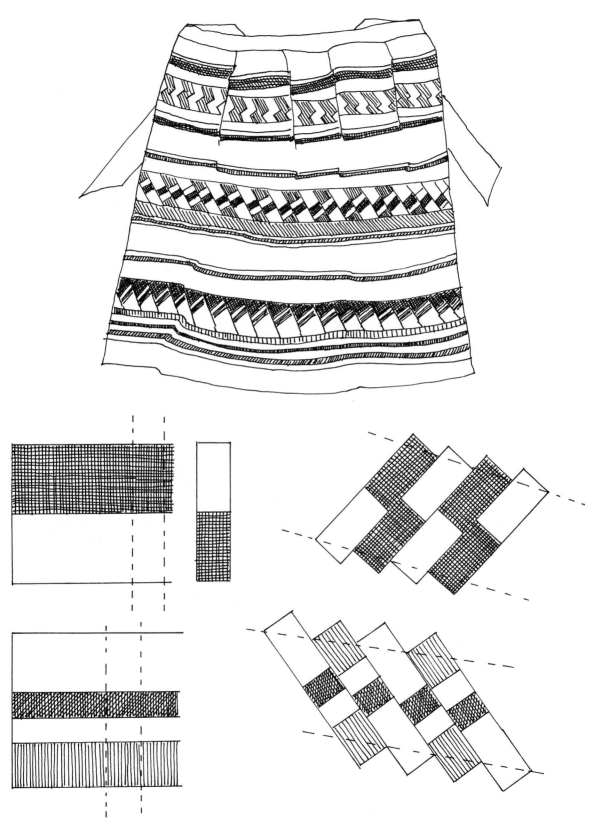

Figure 23   Apron with a row of seminole patchwork.

aprons. The rows of ric-rac braid have given way to the rather more subdued strips of narrow contrasting fabric, mostly appliquéd between the pattern bands, giving a less confusing result.

Many small items can be made and decorated with Seminole bands, perhaps using those left over from a previous piece of work. I have used a Seminole border on an apron (figure 23) which has pockets constructed in quite a different manner.

The oven cloth in figure 24 I found for sale in England. It seems to be an authentic Seminole piece of work, perhaps brought back as a holiday souvenir. The bright colours would ensure that it didn't get mislaid in the kitchen!

Figure 25   Cushion with Seminole band. See diagram 28.

Figure 26   Cushion with Seminole band. See diagram 34c.

Figure 24   Oven cloth, 18 cm x 24 cm (7 in. x 9 in.).

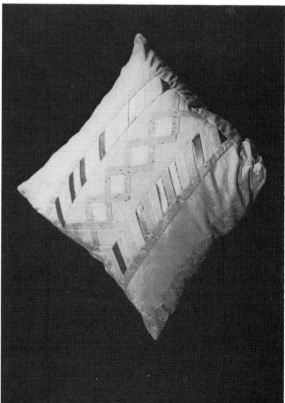

The two cushions, in figures 25 and 26, made as a matching pair in pale pastel colours, contain two pattern bands from Chapter 5, see diagrams 28 (page 40) and 34c (page 46).

Figure 27   Zip bag.

Corduroy and cotton give textural interest to the zip bag (figure 27). This bag was the result of another project. Following the Seminole tradition of making long lengths of pattern bands for later use (figure 5, page 21), I found that by cutting and adding to the already made band various combinations would emerge. The two place mats in blue and white (figure 28) use the simple but effective pattern described in Chapter 4, diagram 17.

Figure 28   Two table mats made by Jean Birse.

Chapter Eight

Medallion quilts

For the American colonists patchwork was a way of using or re-using scraps of clothing or other leftover fabric, to make a cover for a bed which could then be lined and padded and quilted. Thus the technique developed of pieces cut and joined one at a time to make the spectacular patterns which we associate with American quilts.

Seminole patchwork differs in all respects from this approach. New fabric is always used, making it possible to cut the long strips for the pattern bands. The colour combinations are of an intensity that would have shocked the colonists. Although the strip method had been used before, the Seminoles were the first to use its possibilities with such ingenuity. Their unique and precise methods have only been employed in the making of clothes. New clothes are made for tribal ceremonies such as the Green Corn Dance — a yearly festival — but in the main the Indians now make their clothing for the tourist market. There was an attempt several years ago to copyright some of the earlier patterns but this did not succeed. One now sees printed versions of these patterns on many commercial items, such as sheets, pillowcases and clothes, but it is the quality that results from the technique that gives us the textural quality, not only the pattern.

Although the Seminole use their technique of patchwork in horizontal bands of pattern, I have found that the technique lends itself particularly well to the making of medallion quilts, that is to say, those that start with a central block and use different pattern bands working outwards from the centre.

The two medallion quilts illustrated in plates 8 and 12 use a variety of pattern bands, some of which are composed of blocks organized into a pattern band. 'Seminole I' quilt (plate 8) has a central square, composed of folded ribbon blocks, with seven pattern bands surrounding it. For the strips of the folded ribbon blocks I used a 5 cm (2 in.) template. The width of template for cutting the strip band into units is approximately 7 cm (2¾ in.). Allowing for a 5 mm (¼ in.) seam allowance, the strip after seaming will be about 4 cm (1½ in.). The method used is described in pattern band 7, diagram 19 (page 29). To achieve a three-dimensional effect I have used a light central strip in one band, and a dark central strip in the other. Figures 29 and 29a show the placing of each unit, and the result when seamed. There are 32 units in the central square.

Adjacent to the centre we have one of the most popular pattern bands used by the Seminole. Instructions are given in diagram 17 (page 28). I have used three different strip bands to enable three different colours to be used for the central strip. The units are seamed together keeping to a regular order. The same template is used as for the ribbon blocks (5 cm).

The second band, consisting of nine patch blocks, is separated from its predecessor by an unpieced strip of fabric so that the blocks are kept separate from the preceding pattern band and do not merge into it. Diagram 39 (page 50) gives the instructions for the nine patch blocks, once again using the 5 cm (2 in.) template.

To separate each block I have used an unpieced unit. Since I have used only two colours for the blocks, interspersions, and the separating strip, the effect is quite different to that of the nine-patch blocks which make up each corner. The method of construction is exactly the same, but the different colour scheme produces a larger looking block (see figure 31).

A chevron border follows the nine-patch block border, using two tones for the central strip to give a three-dimensional effect, as in figure 10 (page 32). See also diagram 19 (page 29). The fourth band is a repeat of the first, but instead of several

Figure 29a   Two strip bands with different coloured middle strips, marked ready for cutting. See diagram 5.

Figure 29b   Units from the strip bands cut and placed ready for seaming, with resulting block.

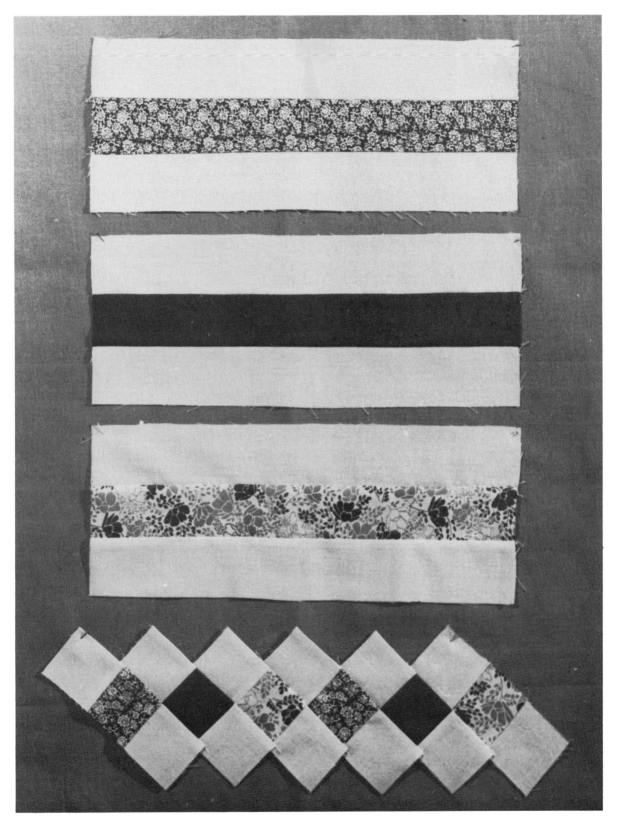

*Figure 30   Three different strip bands from which to cut the
units for the pattern band. Diagram 17.*

Figure 32   The use of the same fabric for the adjoining strips of these three pattern bands eliminates the straight seam line that would otherwise be apparent.

Figure 31   Different versions of the same nine patch block showing the effect of different tonal values. Diagram 39.

colours for the central strip I have only used one; see diagram 17 (page 28). The fifth band is a wide chevron border using four strips; see diagram 20 (page 31). Note that the first and last band are of the same fabric as that which joins it on the two adjacent bands (figure 32). This disguises the straight seam and gives a more lively effect.

The penultimate border is another nine-patch block, set on the diagonal. See diagram 4 (page 17). I have used a wider central strip as described in diagram 40 (page 57).

For the last border two strip bands were made, using an identical sequence of fabric for the strips in each. The width of the finished border is measured out on both strip bands and cut in opposite directions; see diagram 5 (page 18). The 45° angle will enable the corners to be accurately turned (see figure 33). The triangular pattern in the centre of each side is effected by cutting away the excess material before joining with a straight seam (see figure 34).

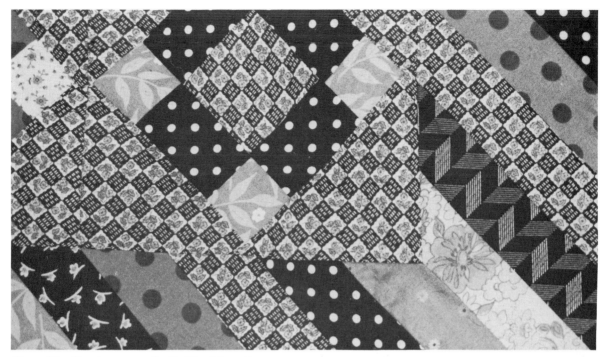

*Figure 33   Turning corner of quilt. The 45° enables the two
sides to fit round the corner.*

*Figure 34   Triangular pattern in the centre of each side
formed by cutting away excess fabric.*

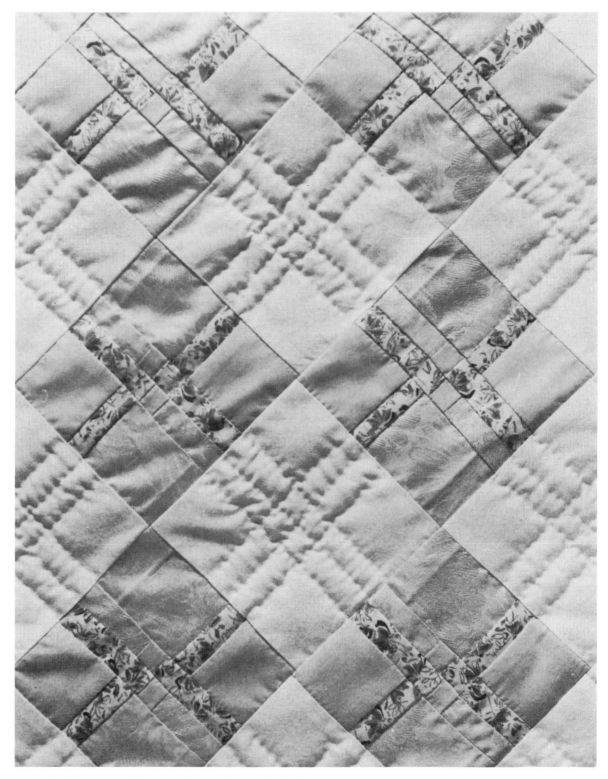

*Figure 35   Central blocks in 'Field of Gold' quilt (plate 12)
set on the diagonal. Plain squares are quilted with the
shadow pattern of the pieced blocks. See diagram 44 for block
pattern.*

In the other medallion quilt, plate 12, I have used very pale colours, which are not typical of actual Seminole work. The quilt is called 'Field of Gold'. Unbleached calico and a variety of fabrics varying from gold to orange are used. The central block is not a square as in 'Seminole I'; therefore as the pattern bands surrounding it are of equal width, the resulting quilt is oblong, a more suitable shape for a single bed than a square.

The central oblong consists of twelve pieced blocks, set on the diagonal. Requiring only two strip bands, the first block of the series in diagram 44 (page 56) explains the method of construction. The plain areas between are quilted with a shadow pattern of the pieced block (figure 35). Each block measures 9.5 cm (3¾ in.) when finished. Seven pattern bands surround the central oblong, separated in some instances with plain strips.

The pattern band adjacent to the centre (figure 36) is described in Chapter Three, diagram 14 (page 25). This two-strip band is composed of strips each measuring 7.5 cm (approx. 2¾ in.). The template used for cutting into units is narrower than this, 4 cm (1½ in.). A very simple pattern band of strips makes up the second border (Chapter Two, diagram 7, page 17), with a block in each corner. This block pattern is used again for the fourth border. Although the method of construction of this block pattern is not, as far as I know, one used by the Seminole, I will include instructions for making it in this chapter, because it is so quick and efficient.

Figure 36 A two strip band, called 'Lightning' by the Seminole. See diagram 14.

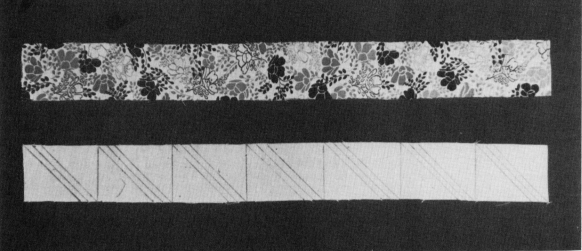

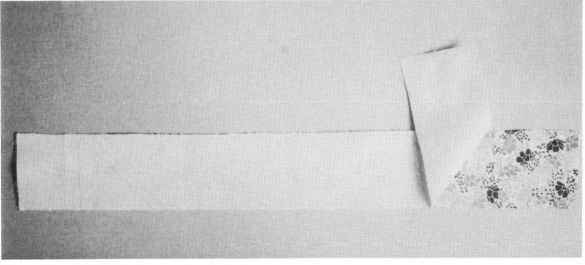

Figure 37 **a-h** *Method of construction for block pattern used in border no. 4 of the 'Field of Gold' quilt.*

82

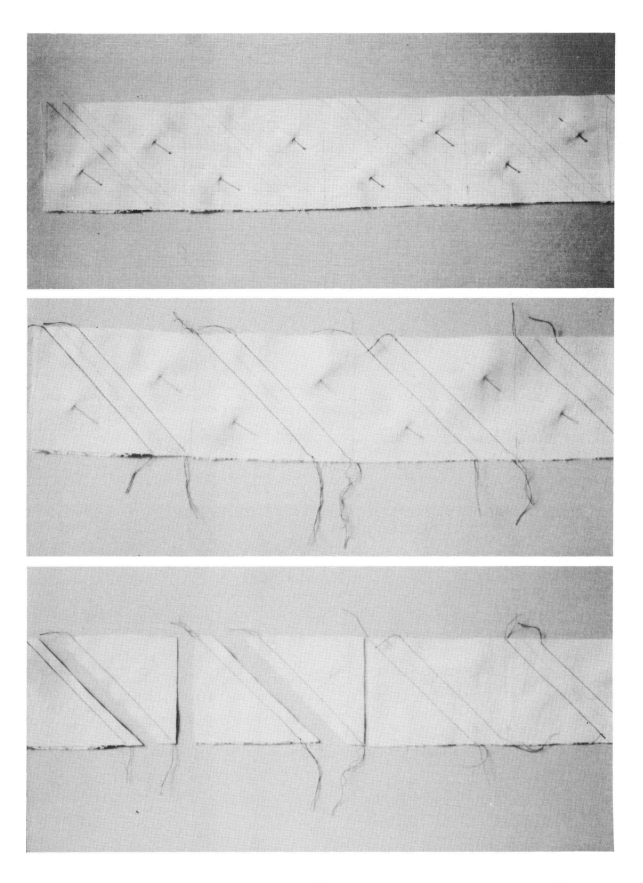

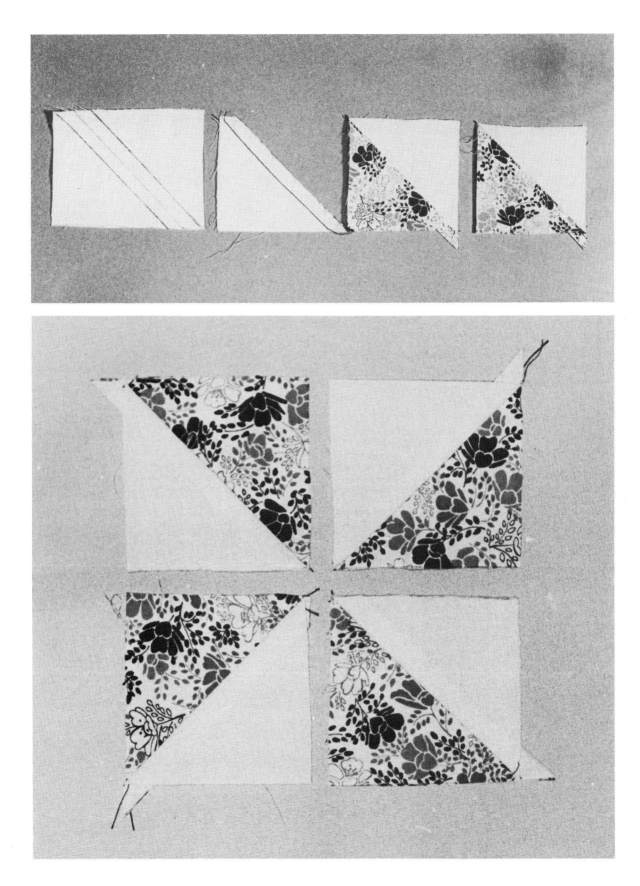

Two strips are needed of identical width, but different colours (figure 37a). I have used a template of 7 cm (2¾ in.). On the wrong side of one strip, measure the width (7 cm) along one edge and draw the diagonal from this point. From this line add two seam allowances. Draw a vertical line from the point at which the last line meets the edge of the strip (figure 37b). Continue to mark in this way along the length of the strip. When this is done place the two strips one on top of the other, right sides together, marked strip uppermost (figure 37c). Pin at intervals (figure 37d). Machine stitch the two strips together along the two outer diagonal lines (figure 37e). The centre line is not sewn.

Cut the strip on the central diagonal, between the two lines of stitching, and on the vertical (figure 37f). Press out to form a square (figures 37g). One unit can be used to make a pattern band of triangles as in border no. 3 of the Field of Gold quilt, figure 38. Or, four units will make the windmill block (figure 37h) used in border no. 4.

Figure 38 Border of triangles, using method described in figure 37.

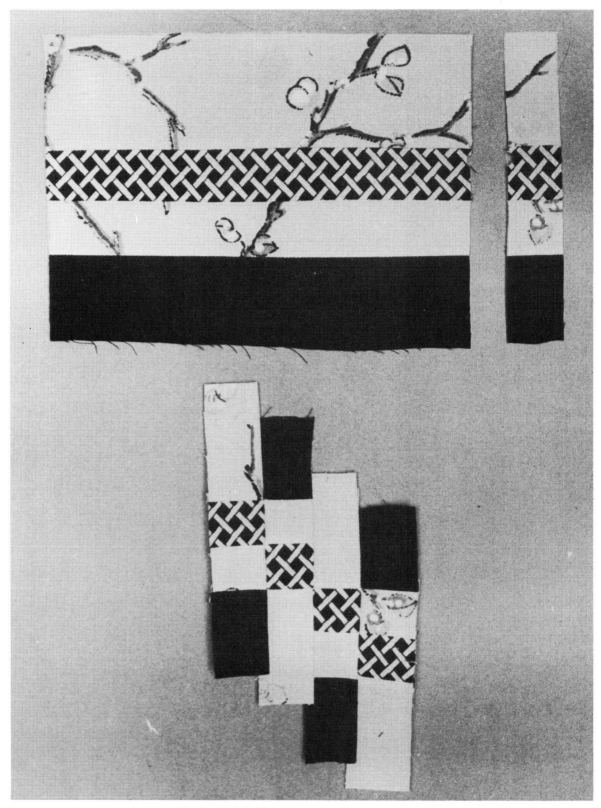

*Figure 39   The strip band needed for 'Field of Gold' quilt,
border no. 5, and units arranged prior to trimming.*

Border no. 5 is a variation of the strip band shown in diagram 24 (page 37). The difference is that the lower strip is narrower, not the same as the upper strip. Figure 39 indicates this, and the way to arrange the units. After a plain separating strip a saw tooth pattern band (figure 40) makes border no. 6 (see diagram 23, page 35). So that the straight seam line is not apparent, the same fabric is used in one of the strips in the next pattern band, border no. 7. This is a three-strip band (see diagram 18, page 28) with the narrow middle strip made of a satin type fabric. The same fabric separates border nos 6 and 7 with a very narrow strip, before the most popular pattern band in the Seminole repertoire (diagram 17, page 28) is used.

A saw tooth border is the last one, no. 8. Once again it uses the same fabric adjacent to the previous border to disguise the straight line of the seam.

Figures 41a, b and 42a, b are further examples of medallion quilts. Both make use of the interlacing block for the central panel. See Chapter Six, diagram 43. As the fabrics used in both are patterned and very pale, the total effect does not have the vibrant quality associated with Seminole work, but a quiet and restful result has been achieved instead.

Figure 40   Finished border no. 5 in 'Field of Gold' quilt.

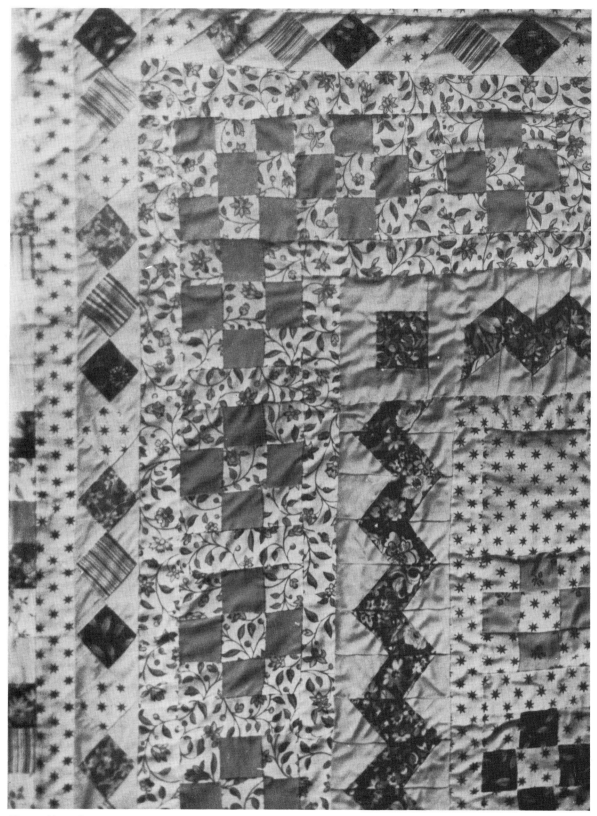

*Figure 41a   Centre panel of a medallion quilt made by Liz
Paton. See diagram 43.*

Figure 41b   Surrounding borders of Liz Paton's quilt.

Figure 42a   Part of quilt made by Trudi; the very pale patterned material tends to obscure the design.

Figure 42b   Borders of quilt by Trudi.

Specialist Suppliers for patchwork

UK

The Patchwork Dog and the Calico Cat
21 Chalk Farm Road
London NW1

Strawberry Fayre Fabrics
Chagford
Devon TQ13 8EN

All large department stores will hold a good stock of suitable materials.

US

It would be difficult to provide a fully up-to-date list of patchwork suppliers covering all parts of the USA. Readers are therefore referred to *The Quilter's Catalog: A Complete Guide to Quilting Sources and Supplies* by Linda Stokes (Main Street Press, New Jersey).

Suggestions for further reading

Publications

DUDLEY, Taimi, *Strip Patchwork*, Van Nostrand Reinhold Company, New York, 1980

RUSH, Beverley, with WITTMAN, Lassie, *The Complete Book of Seminole Patchwork*, Madrona Publishers, Seattle, 1982

Seminole Men's Clothing a paper by Dr William Sturtevant, curator of North American Ethnology, Smithsonian Institute
(This and other essays by Dr Sturtevant can be studied at the library of the Museum of Mankind.)

Museums

The museums listed below contain examples of Seminole patchwork, although the collections are not always out on display. It is usually possible to request permission to see items, especially if proof of serious interest can be given.

UK

Museum of Mankind
Ethnographic Department of British Museum
6 Burlington Gardens
London W1X 2EX

Apart from the Museum of Mankind, there are no sizeable collections of Seminole patchwork in the UK.

USA

Museum of the American Indian
3401 Bruckner Boulevard
Bronx
New York 10461

The Florida State Museum
University of Florida
Museum Road
Gainesville 32611

Heard Museum
22 East Monte Vista Road
Phoenix
Arizona 85004

Historical Association of Southern Florida
Metro Dade Cultural Centre
101 West Flagler Street
Miami
Florida 33130

Smithsonian Museum of Natural History
Constitutional Avenue
Washington DC 205060

Index

offsetting 20, 27, 36
Oklahoma 10, 38

paper 21
pattern bands 19, 21, 22, 28, 30, 38, 60, 72, 75
patterned 15, 87
pincushions 65
plain 15
proportions 19, 22, 42, 52, 57
protractor 19
puckered 15

quilting 42, 65, 75, 81

railroad 10
rectangular 14
reservations 10, 67
ribbon 55, 75
ric-rac 72, 41

samples 22
saw tooth 26, 34, 87
Scottish Highlanders 59
seam allowances 15, 48, 85
seams 16, 17, 19, 65
second seam 42
set square 19
sewing machine 10, 15, 17, 59
shells 38
slaves 9, 10, 50
Spain 9
spider web strip 25

strips 14, 16, 19, 21, 22, 25, 26, 28, 33, 34, 48, 51, 52, 65, 75, 85
strip bands 16, 17, 19, 25, 27, 28, 34, 36, 41, 48, 57, 65, 81, 87
symbolic 38
symmetrical 57

Tamiami Trail 10, 59, 67
Tampa 59
Tampa Bay 10
tearing fabric 14
templates 14, 15, 18, 20, 22, 25, 28, 75
three-dimensional 30, 55, 75
tonal values 30, 51, 57
tones 41, 52, 75
tourists 10, 59, 67, 75
traders 10, 59
trading post 10
traditional 13, 38, 42, 49, 59, 67
transitional 59
triangles 26, 34, 85
triangular 14, 20
trousers 59
tucks 62, 65

units 14, 16, 17, 19, 20, 21, 22, 27, 34, 38, 40, 42, 57, 62, 65, 75, 87

washing 15, 16
white pencil 15, 19
women 10, 13, 20, 52, 59, 60, 67